B/RODI

Born in Gillingham Kent in 1948, Jacki Rodikis was educated at Chatham Grammar School for Girls. She trained as a computer programmer, and then developed a successful business. She is passionate about raising public awareness of the long term effects of childhood sexual abuse and has recently established 'Women for Change', a charity to help women survivors. She has three children, and four grandchildren and now lives in South Warwickshire.

www.jacki-rodikis.co.uk

BECAUSE YOU'RE A WOMAN

Jacki Rodikis

BECAUSE YOU'RE A WOMAN

AUSTIN & MACAULEY

A CIP catalogue record for this title is
available from the British Library.

ISBN 978 1 905609 74 1

www.austinmacauley.com

First Published (2010)
Austin & Macauley Publishers Ltd.
25 Canada Square
Canary Wharf
London
E14 5LB

Printed & Bound in Great Britain

DEDICATION

For my children and grandchildren

"No matter what happens, keep on beginning and failing.
Each time you fail, start all over again, and you will grow
stronger until you find that you have accomplished a purpose
– not the one you began with perhaps, but one you will be
glad to remember.

Anne Sullivan (American teacher 1866-1936)

ACKNOWLEDGEMENTS

Special thanks are due to the staff of the Cardinal Clinic who first encouraged me to use writing as a way of expressing my turbulent emotions. I shall be ever grateful to Jenny Becker who read through my initial tentative drafts and told me to 'go for it'. Her time and interest spent in patient correction of my poor grammar was invaluable. Very many thanks must go also to Marlene Hickin. Ever mindful of my history, she nevertheless firmly marked passages that were redundant to the main thrust of the story, and her 'red lines' honed the manuscript until it became the book you are about to read. But my most heartfelt gratitude must go to my daughter Kate, whose love and constancy of encouragement gave me the confidence to keep going and follow through to the end.

For those and for my friends who have stood firm through this journey:-

"Oh, the comfort, the inexpressible comfort, of feeling safe with a person; having neither to weigh thoughts or measure words, but to pour them all out just as they are, chaff and grain together, knowing that a faithful hand will take and sift them, keep what is worth keeping, and then, with the breath of kindness, blow the rest away."

George Eliot (Mary Ann Evans) (1819-1880)

"Who knows what women can be when they are finally free to become themselves?"

Betty Freidman (b. 1921) American feminist and writer

PART 1: DADDY

Where do I start, how do I begin to tell of this singular journey that has been my life? How do we untangle the confusing mix of loving, joy, hurt and pain that is the inheritance of our lives, and why do we expect so much and find so little, in the fragile relationships that we build or are born into?

We are thrust naked from the warmth and security of our mother's womb, and begin our journey in innocence, untouched and unsullied by the darkness that lives alongside us in the world, dependent on those around us to mould and guide and protect until we are ready to take control and choose our own direction. Those guardians are responsible for the foundation upon which we will build the model that is our lives. A foundation that must be strong and resilient if we are to have any chance of thriving through the trials that life will surely throw at us. But theirs is not the sole impact on the design that will become our life's journey. Even before our birth the blueprint is determined, the journey begun and the path chosen.

In The Beginning...

In that tiny moment of time
That split second
That final, gasping, sweating, heaving moment of passion
When I was conceived

Destiny stepped in with her coin
Tossed
And my fate was sealed

Two 'X' chromosomes
Fusing to the female form

Nothing mysterious or beautiful
Just a chemical reaction

And I was created.

CHAPTER 1

Married in April 1947, my parents had only one short month together before my father was sent to the Middle East with the Royal Signals Army Corp. Perhaps I was conceived the night before he left as an unwilling conscriptee, boarding ship for a faraway destination, an insecure young man, newly wed and wanting only to cement his marriage and new role as husband.

It must have been a shock for my father reading the handwritten letter, as he sat in his desert tent in Egypt, learning of the impending arrival of a baby. How welcome months later, was the news of the arrival of his daughter? An intruder into that new and fragile relationship, now metamorphosised into something totally different to the one he had been forced to leave. How did he feel all those long months away? His own mother had died giving birth to him. Was he afraid that he would lose his young wife? Was he already jealous of me, able to enjoy the warmth and intimacy that he was being denied, curled deep within her in the warmth and safety of her womb, and then held in her arms, cuddled and caressed and much loved? Demanding her every attention whilst he was so far away, out of control, out of touch and unable to make his needs and wishes known.

My mother stayed with her parents, comfortably at home in a leafy avenue of terraced houses in Gillingham, Kent, and it was in a maternity nursing home only two streets away that I was born the following February in one of the harshest winters on record. Twenty foot snowdrifts were recorded, and ice bound ships were unable to deliver coal and food to the country. My mother, Marion, was just 22. Letters flew back and forth between England and Egypt, until finally two crossed, both with the name "Jacqueline".

I am told that my grandfather adored me; that he could not bear to hear me cry, and that he spoiled me. Why not? I was his first grandchild. His own childhood had been passed in a Children's Cottage Home, because his mother, a single parent in the early 1900s, had been forced to hand him into care. His children had been born during the tough long years of depression before the war, a time of tremendous financial struggle. He had, of necessity, travelled long distances to get work and worked long hours, taking any job he could to keep his young family fed and clothed. There was no dole or social security payments, no family income support system. If you had no job, you had no money. So it was understandable that he would want to give his first grandchild all the love, fussing and protection that he had never received, nor had the time and energy to give to his own children.

My mother's younger brother, Edward, was still living at home when I was born. He was sixteen and training to be a printer. He has told me that he would often lift me from my cot early in the morning, and take me downstairs to the scullery to make the morning tea, sharing a biscuit with me whilst waiting for the kettle to sing on the gas stove.

It is such a pity that I cannot recall those very early months of life in my grandparents' house. They would be very precious memories of a time when I knew I was loved without condition. I have a photograph of myself aged about seven months, sitting in the garden on a pink blanket, dressed in a white knitted cardigan, probably made by my grandmother. For most of her life, until arthritis set in, she would have some knitting in a bag beside her armchair. My hair is blonde, framing a face that I cannot recognize as my own. Are they my eyes? Is that my mouth? Are those tiny chubby hands really mine? In the photograph I am looking up at someone, smiling in anticipation. I don't know why, but somewhere deep inside I believe it must have been my grandfather. On the back of the photograph it says 'Fluffy – Summer 1948'.

I must have been very contented living in the house that was later to become my only refuge in a very lonely world. To me it will always be a wonderful house, full of vivid memories of childhood games of make believe and dressing up, of delicious smells of home baked cakes and apple pie, of big soft feather beds, warmed with hot water bottles on a winter's night. A pervading smell of Palmolive soap filled the house, except in my grandmother's bedroom, where the air held the lingering perfume of her Ponds cold cream; all she ever used on her face, which was soft and clear until the day she died. The senses' recollections are strong, and tears still fill my eyes when those fondest and dearest memories are woken from their slumber by these passing perfumes. In the fireplace, on the hearth in the kitchen, sat two brass Buddhas. They now sit next to the wood-burning stove in the little room at home where I work; two treasured, physical reminders of that almost magical house, providing a tangible link with the few cherished memories of the happier times of my childhood.

CHAPTER 2

As I was born in February 1948, and my younger brother, Anthony David, in November 1949 my father must have returned home before I was one year old. Though the original length of National Service had been increased in December 1948 from one year to eighteen months, he had been able to obtain a discharge on medical grounds. Physically my father was perfectly healthy and my understanding is that his discharge was due to mental instability. I wonder what the dynamics were of the various relationships in that house: five adults living together with a small baby.

My grandparents, Edward and Florence, were simple folk, born in 1902 and 1903; a generation that only knew hard work, and war. They had met in Kensington, London whilst in service. They fell in love and my mother was born on 19th January 1926, the result of their illicit amour. They married in September 1925, the abandoned little boy and the seventh child of a bargee, and worked and strived to provide a home for their young family – my uncle arriving four years after my mother – and they remained very much in love until the end of their lives.

I know from odd comments heard much later in my life that my grandparents had never taken to my father, and I can imagine that his return from the Middle East must have caused many a ripple in the calm of their domestic life. He would have needed to re-establish himself as the head of his family group: a wife and new baby. This new controlling influence over mother and baby would have clashed with my grandfather's position as man of the house, and hitherto provider of care and protection for mother and child. I know how cruel my father can be in his spoken words, and I doubt very much that he would have shown any tact in his handling of this uncomfortable situation. The house was large enough to accommodate the new young family, but soon after my brother was born, my father succeeded in jumping the housing queue by convincing the authorities that his mother-in-law was making life extremely difficult for him, and that their living conditions were cramped. I cannot imagine my grandmother making life difficult for anyone. She was incapable of deceit, enmity or connivance, whereas I have learnt only too well that my father is capable of all three.

I have no recollection of the move to our new house, on a council estate in Rochester, or of those early years of my brother's life. But the safe and cosy world that I lived in had already started to disintegrate. My aunt Margaret has been my source of information about the family history. She had married my uncle when I was eleven and had spent a lot of time with my grandmother. She had been told that, whereas my grandfather would pick me up from my cot and cuddle me when I cried, my father would hold me down and try by sheer force to get me to sleep. What must I have felt at this sudden change, at this new and forceful pair of hands, this previously unknown presence, which was not comforting but frightening?

Unlike the memories of my grandparents' house, those of my parents' are not warm and cosy, with good smells and sensations. Memories are of a cold house – I am only able to feel it as a winter house – the rooms a succession of boxes where all activities were governed by my father's strict regime. Our bedrooms, the bathroom – nowhere could offer a private space in which we could create our own world of warmth and comfort. The small bathroom overlooked the rear garden; the basin situated under a window that was always opened early in the morning, even in winter when the garden and distant fields were white and frosty. Skinny and shivering, wearing only thin cotton vests we hurriedly washed our faces and brushed our teeth, desperate to return to the relative warmth of our bedrooms to dress. I suppose the simplest way to convey our lifestyle was that the house was run like an army camp, with minimal physical comforts, strict bedtimes and mealtimes, and controlled activities. Sunday evening was always bath night, even when we were much older. I can remember a shocking row one Sunday when I was seventeen, and my father had insisted that I went up for my bath at 5.00pm. The one and only positive aspect of this clockwork regime was that we always knew what time he would be going out to the pub, and we could experience a short period of relief from the constant tension under which we lived. Neither was my mother excluded from his domination. Though I was not conscious of her ever being told what to do, I know that she fell in with my father's wishes even though on occasions that meant that she was not protecting her children from his cruel behaviour.

My parents live in that house to this day; fifty-eight years of memories bouncing off the walls, and out of hidden corners, confronting and accusing, though it maybe that theirs are not the same as mine. Perhaps they have compacted, selected and erased memories until only the simple, happier ones remain, with no obligation to examine or question.

I cannot remember laughter being a spontaneous part of our family group, or the loving closeness within which families can share jokes and tease each other, where weaknesses or worries can be exposed without fear of derision. A child who lives in fear of a parent suffers a betrayal of trust that is devastating in its long-term effects. How can she ever learn to trust if the birthright of a loving and protecting parent is missing or withheld, leaving her to wander in a wilderness of uncertainty, never sure whether it is her that is loved, or what she gives? I look at a photograph of that little girl – presumably an early school photograph, shyly looking out at the photographer from deep-set eyes, smiling softly and I wonder what he had said to make her smile in that way? Every time I look at the picture tears come into my eyes. What is still hidden deep within my soul that makes the woman cry when she sees the child?

THE FEAR

She sits in the bath
Naked, a skinny little girl
Shivering

Is it cold?
The open window allows a draught into the bare white room
Whispering around her small body
Sitting, cowering, in the permitted two inches of warm water

Is it the cold air that leaves her shivering?
Or is it something else
Some unvoiced fear?

No comfort in the warm bathwater
Hands clutching her knees to her chest
Eyes fixed on the door, slightly ajar
As the sound of approaching footsteps on the stairs
Brings another shiver

Oh please, please let it be Mummy

The door opens
'Mummy is busy so I will bath you tonight'

Her heart sinks, her body shrinking inward
Trying to disappear, to be wiped from view
But still she obediently stands
Waiting to be soaped down

No flannel or facecloth
Not for her the dignity of washing her own body
Just his soapy hands
Sliding all over her tiny, flat body – no curves
Not a single part that is hers to care for

His soapy finger – pushing, probing and rubbing between her
legs

'Doesn't that feel nice?'

'No' – screams the voice in her head
'It stings, it hurts, it doesn't feel nice
And I don't want you to touch me there!'

But her mouth does not open
The cry unspoken
The hurt unvoiced, denied

Instead, she looks at the man
Dumbly acquiescent

This is my daddy
And I want him to love me

CHAPTER 3

Other than the abuse I can only recall unconnected incidents belonging to the period of my early childhood. I find it difficult to link them through any specific sequences of age or time. However, small blocks of memory have been uncovered through therapy. Gentle massaging of the psyche produces some shocking results, and feelings from a hitherto unremembered moment in childhood can suddenly find expression through an adult mind.

I can see a small sandpit about half way down the garden on the right hand side of a narrow path that runs from the bottom of the steps outside the kitchen door to the far end of the garden. A little girl squats and digs in the sandpit; a little girl with short, light brown hair, wearing a frock, white socks and sandals. She is hunkered down on her haunches; knees almost meeting her shoulders, concentrating on her work, and alongside is a pet dog, a black and brown mongrel. I reach into this memory, into my deep subconscious, and become the child and can sense the dog patiently watching me, maybe waiting for his turn to dig. The sun is warm on my shoulders, but I sense dampness more by smell than touch. I become aware of an adult presence; a dark shape approaches and overshadows the sunny spot where the little girl digs. Instead of reaching up in anticipation of the pleasure of being gathered into loving arms, she wets herself. I can feel the dampness of warm, wet knickers against her skin and I can feel her shame; hot tears on her cheeks.

Though quiet and shy I was bright, and learnt quickly, moving up through the classes at school faster than some of my contemporaries. Our estate boasted a brand new school complex, built over a hill; the plateau at the highest point of the hill opposite the bottom of our road, with the infant school on one downward slope and the junior school the other. The infant school had attracted the least investment of the two, and consisted of two rows of pre-fabricated huts, like

Nissan huts; grey-green in colour, which sat along the slope of the hill like two strings of fat sausages.

First class was held in the first hut along the bottom row, second in the next, and so on until you reached the top, physically and educationally.

Though I cannot remember much of my time at the Infant School, there is one incident that sticks out in my mind. I recall poking my tongue out at the teacher, an act totally out of character, as I have always been fearful of figures in authority. I must have been in the first or second class because I picture the classroom as being on the lower level, near the school gate. I can still feel the dreadful shame of being hauled out in front of a class full of children and forced to stand behind the upright piano. Perhaps though this was an early indication of my rebellious streak.

Neither can I remember any friends from this age. I do know that I stood at the edge of the playground on my own watching the games of tag and hopscotch. Not confident enough to run and join in with the other children with that natural uninhibited exuberance of childhood, I would stand there feeling that I had nothing to offer that they might want, nothing of value that might allow me inclusion into their close knit group. I had already internalised that to belong, to be wanted, I had to give something. I know I felt different to the other children. I realise now that I knew things that they didn't, and had experienced things far beyond anything that they had or were likely to and this set me apart from them. But I had not yet made this leap of understanding. I just felt insignificant and unwanted, and I envied those who could so easily run in and become a part of the game.

My brother Tony was only two years behind me, but I don't recall that we had a great deal of contact with each other during school time. At home it was another matter. We were partners in crime, or rather his crime. Not motivated as I was to work hard, he did the minimum necessary to get by. He was always in trouble with my father, and a frequent punishment was to be sent to bed without his tea. Many is the time that I crept quietly up the stairs to his bedroom carrying a plate of jam sandwiches and a glass of milk, hoping that I would not be caught out by our parents who had settled in the sitting room for the evening.

One particular night I remember, my father intended thrashing Tony with his belt for some misdemeanour he had committed. He enlisted the aid of a neighbour from a family that we were at the time quite friendly with. Mr Collins held me, struggling and fighting against him, in the dining room, while in the kitchen my father administered the punishment. I had a sense that Mr Collins was not entirely happy with his role, because he tried to calm and soothe me rather than simply physically holding me down. I cannot remember the reason for the thrashing, just the fact that I knew it to be unjust. I would have fought tooth and nail to protect my little brother if I had been allowed to. My instinctive reaction to Tony's suffering was not to cower and pretend it wasn't happening, but to fight against the injustice of it. This fighting spirit remained alive in me, and was perhaps the part of my character that gave me some resilience to the abuse that I was suffering.

My bedroom was at the front of the house overlooking the front door. It was no more than a box-room, space only for a small dressing table, and a single bed pushed up against the wall adjoining my parents' room. Below the window was a small concrete porch, supported by two metal poles. On a summer's evening, after being banished to his bedroom, Tony would climb out of my bedroom window, lower himself to the porch roof with my assistance and shimmy down the pole to go and play with his friends. How he got back in, and whether he was caught, I have no idea. But it was typical of our relationship that I would help him to outwit our father to escape the often over-severe punishments that were meted out to him.

SHARING

The bright, tinkling tune of the ice cream van
Ringing outside in the street
Two children
Brother and sister
Rush to the window
Pushing the net curtains to one side
Please Mummy, please can we have one
Just today
For a special treat

Clutching the sixpenny piece
The little girl
Older
More responsible of the two
Runs along the path to the rear of the van
The friendly man asking
What would you like
Pet?
Two please, cornets, plain three-penny

Handing over the sixpenny piece
Taking delivery of the two precious cones
Stepping back onto the pavement
She takes a lick
Before starting to walk
Back to the house
Carrying carefully the delight soon to be savoured

Plop!
One perfect orb of white frosty cream
Drops to the pavement
Was it the one she licked?

Arriving at the door, at the rear of the house
Where the smaller child

Little brother
Trusting her to deliver the precious cargo
Stands and waits patiently
Anticipating the taste of cold, creamy delight

She hands him the empty cone

Sorry
But yours fell out!

CHAPTER 4

In June 1954, my mother was rushed into hospital as a result of life-threatening complications with her third pregnancy; my brother Robert consequently being born prematurely. I have a wonderful recollection of her returning home with our new baby brother. She is standing in the doorway between the hall and the kitchen, dressed in her favourite black suit, holding our new brother, a mass of white shawl enveloping her arms, and flowing down to her knees. She looks very happy, beautiful even.

I loved my new baby brother very much. A captive audience, here was someone who had no choice in bearing my company. Unable to speak or to control my movements, he could not leave me feeling unworthy. Here was an opportunity, unique and separate from all the confusing signals that they were receiving, for my natural female instincts to surface and react as they were designed to. What a joy it was to be safely ensconced on the large sofa with Robert propped up on a pillow in my small child's arms, carefully holding a bottle of milk and tentatively feeding this wonderful new friend.

I moved up to the junior school in September 1954, when my baby brother was three months old, and I was six and a half. As far as I can recall there were no set tests to examine your ability to cope with the demands of junior school work; it was an automatic move for the rising sevens. Though the junior school was geographically close to the infant school it presented a whole new world to me. A world of large, bright, airy classrooms, long corridors with polished floors, an enormous school hall where every morning assembly was held, and large expanses of playing fields and playgrounds.

My first year teacher, Miss Rogers, was the only lady teacher I had at this school. I enjoyed learning, worked hard and achieved good results, evident in my reports, which I still have – carefully preserved documents marking my progress through young life. If I did not achieve an 'A'+1 I was disappointed, bitterly. Already I had become a perfectionist, constantly setting myself high standards, pushing myself to the limits of my ability, not understanding then that I was reacting to the betrayal of childhood's trust and dependence; developing the belief that I was not loved or lovable by just being 'me', but had to please others in order to receive love. There was no 'me', just another's toy. Love was not freely given: it was only received by doing what my father required.

My subsequent teachers were all men. I suppose this could have had an adverse effect on my schoolwork. But I am not aware that at that time I had difficulties in relating to men. I do not think I had a fear or dislike of men in general. All the male teachers were kind to me, and at the end of each year I was terribly upset to leave them to move on. And my grandfather had shown me nothing but love and adoration. The relationship with my father was unique, a thing of itself, separate from any other part of my life despite the appalling subliminal effects it was having on my emotional development. Now, it is frightening to recall the ease with which he was able to make me succumb to his every demand, the misuse of his power so easily developed from my child's trust in him. The adjoining wall between my parents' room and mine became a symbol of the paper-thin divide between my privacy and the ignominy of my surrender to him.

TAPPING

Tap, Tap, Tap
Steady, repeated noises
Insistent
The summons
Calling me
Tapping
On the wall
Beside me

Bury my head beneath the covers
Trying to blank it out
Or ignore it
But it keeps on going

Louder
Persistent tapping
Dripping onto my head
Like Chinese water torture
I am fixed
And cannot escape it
Drilling into my head
Through the covers,
Through my hands

I wish it would stop
I wish I were deaf

Finally I give in
Reluctantly creeping from my bed
I look at the wall
Helpless
Resigned

And yet
Why should I

Why cannot I stay
Warm in bed
Enjoy the Saturday morning lie in
Alone

Moving slowly
Reluctantly
Through the doorway
Around the corner
Into their bedroom
But they are not there

He is
Lifting the covers for me to crawl in
Beside him

Sick
Frightened
Stiff little body
Obeying the whispered commands

The door opens
She moves into the room
Opens the cupboard
Putting away the linen
Ironing finished
Early Saturday morning duty done
Leaving her day free

Mummy
Please stop this

But she does not hear
The words not screamed
As they should be
Not uttered
Not even whispered
They remain

Locked inside my head

Eyes beseeching
Sending a wordless message

Please Mummy, please

"What are you two up to?"
Laughing
She turns away
Her back to the little girl
Ignoring the pleading eyes
Unheeding of the screaming
Inside the child's head

The little girl
Her little girl
Me

Who only wants to be
Beside Her

Shortly after moving to the junior school I told my mother that I could not see the writing on the blackboard. My sight was tested and I was found to be very shortsighted. With no spare money for the luxury of bespoke glasses I was given a pair of the round, pink, national health spectacles that were standard issue for children at the time – perfectly rounded, pink wire circles. "Spectacles" – how I hated that word, still do. Picture me – very skinny – legs like matchsticks, wearing sensible, heavy duty, black, lace-up shoes, hair tied up with a ribbon. Four eyes – I must have looked like a miniature version of Olive Oil – but I did not have a Popeye to look out for me. I really did not need this additional blow to my already diminished self-image, to contribute to my developing conviction that I was unattractive, and not a welcome addition to any peer group. So I stood nervously at the edge of the large noisy groups of children, shouting and calling excitedly to each other at break-times.

However my studious and hardworking nature began to pay off. One of my classmates in the second or third year was a very pretty girl called Veronica. She had a dark complexion, and a mass of black curly hair. One term she regularly came to school wearing red patent shoes, the type of shoe that had a patterned, closed front, and one strap and buckle across the front of the ankle. Oh how I admired those pretty red shoes. My serviceable, black lace ups became even more ugly and ungainly on the end of my thin legs when compared to those pretty, little red dancing shoes. Veronica and I reached an arrangement whereby I would give her the answers to her arithmetic, and in return she would allow me to wear her shoes through the morning break. I walked on air in those shoes. Nobody could have felt more beautiful. Sadly, our friendship was short-lived; I think she moved away. Certainly I do not recall her being around in the last year at the junior school.

Another of my peers found an alternative route to my arithmetic answers. A new girl was given the desk immediately next to mine. I cannot remember her name, but I picture her with a ruddy complexion, and short mid-brown hair; quite a stocky girl I think. Did the teacher feel that I needed a friend, and perhaps somebody new would fit the bill? This new girl would pinch my arm until I showed her the answers. If I tried to hide my work, the pinching would increase becoming more painful until I capitulated. Did my mother notice the bruises, or did I tell her? I cannot remember, but I think that she went to the school to complain, because our desks were subsequently moved around. So to some extent my mother was capable of protecting me.

CHAPTER 5

I have very few memories of Robert as a small child. He was six and a half years younger than me and would have only just started school when I moved on to the grammar school. I know that we always considered him to be our mother's favourite. Maybe because he was to be her last baby it was natural for her to especially cherish him. Robert did not start talking until he was almost three years old. Perhaps this was because Tony and I always knew what he wanted and relayed his needs to my parents. But, despite being my mother's favourite, I don't think he suffered any less than Tony and me from my father's cruel attentions. I have only recently heard some of the details of his ill-treatment from my father; my mother apparently not even having either the willpower or the ability to protect her favourite from the cruelty so arbitrarily inflicted by the man she had chosen to spend her life with.

I have a vivid recollection of a family breakfast, of all of us sitting at the table in the dining room, Robert with a bowl of porridge on the table in front of him. Mealtimes were not the noisy, chatty times that I later enjoyed with my own children, a time when we were all together and able to catch up on each other's news from the day at school or work. My father would not countenance any conversation, and meals were eaten in silence. I don't know what Robert did or said, but my father fetched him an almighty smack around the back of his head, and his face went straight forward like a whiplash into the bowl of porridge. Luckily for Robert, the porridge was not steaming hot; at least I don't recall him being burnt.

Mealtimes were far from enjoyable, but the dining table positioned as it was underneath the window looking out into the garden at least provided some sort of diversion for my brothers. I was not so lucky.

THE VASE

It stands on the windowsill
A perpetual reminder
Secret nods and glances
Indicating its presence
Reminding of the secret

Secret

How can a small cream vase
Delicately patterned with a leaf design
Tender, oval leaves with a centre line
Softly coloured pink and peach
Become such an omnipotent presence
Governing every meal
Taken en famille?

Swallowing her mouthful
Difficult
But better than throwing up
She nervously flicks a glance around the table
Has anyone else noticed
Her mother?
Her brothers?
Seemingly not

But he keeps winking
Nodding, grinning at his joke
Shared
Was it only an hour before
In bed
Upstairs
About the vase
On the windowsill

It looks like you
How?
What does he mean?
Looks like her?
There, here
Touching, showing
Softly coloured, peachy pink
Tender, oval with a centre line

Sometimes, alone in the house
She looks at the vase
Longingly
Wanting to pick it up
Smash it
Destroy it
Crush it to a million tiny pieces
To dust
To nothing
End the torment of every meal
Taken en famille

John, the boy who lived next door, was the same age as me, and we were in the same class at school. We did not get on; he seemed to take delight in poking fun at me and my memory of him is of a boy whose attitude reinforced the opinion I had of myself, that I was unattractive and superfluous. I can still recall vividly the pain from the drawing pin that was left upright on my chair during an art class. I sat down, having been to collect some more paper or paint, and immediately stood up again, smarting with pain, eyes full of tears, and turning round saw his face grinning from ear to ear, the only other person in the room aware of my discomfort and embarrassment. I did not complain to the teacher, or cry out loud. I swallowed hard and tried to continue with my painting. Life hurt awfully at times, and I was learning fast that it was pretty much up to me to cope alone with these bad times.

At the end of every summer term the school pageant was held. A girl was chosen as the pageant queen, usually a very pretty girl, and each class prepared a small play or song and dance routine as a display for the parents who would gather proudly around the edge of the large playing field in anticipation of their offspring's perfect performance. One year I was chosen to be one of the red Indians in our class display. Barefoot, kitted out in short Indian skirts, feathers, and war-paint and carrying rubber tomahawks – the boys' enthusiasm would have rendered anything other than rubber lethal – we were to dance and whoop our way in and out of the 'trees' in a semblance of an Indian war-dance. The 'trees' rustled onto centre stage in the middle of the playing field and stood quietly awaiting our arrival. The elderly gramophone began to play, and out we came, Indian file, hopping from foot to foot in the traditional Indian rhythm, whooping, one hand patting an open mouth, and waving our tomahawks up and down in time to the rhythm of our stamping feet. The whole audience collapsed in gales of laughter. I wanted to die right there and then, wished the earth would swallow me up. Hot tears of mortification ran down my cheeks, as I struggled to maintain the beat and complete the dance. As far as I was concerned, my one and only stage performance had ended in total disaster.

And so ended my time at Delce Junior School. Successfully passing the 11 plus and managing to gain a place at a girls grammar school, I left with a mental note not to indulge in school plays, and to check my seat before sitting down.

CHAPTER 6

Summer was, and still is my favourite time of year. I am sure that part of the reason for this is the opportunities that the warmer weather offered to escape the repressive confines of our home life. Though these new freedoms would not mean that I could fully escape my father's attention, they provided small periods of respite in which joy and laughter could find their way to the surface and be released in an excited bubble of childhood glee.

Most school summer holidays Tony and I would stay at my grandmother's for a week or more, back in that wonderful house where I had spent the first year of my life. I am sure that we must have been a trial to her, but the freedom of expression and thought, and the fun we had at her home have provided me with the few truly happy memories that I have of my childhood. Dressing up in her old clothes and shoes, playing shops with all the groceries tipped out of her cupboards, or making a bus with her dining room chairs; walking round to the local park, and playing for hours on the swings, the maypole and the see-saws. True, Granny scrubbed hard behind our ears at bedtime, but it was worth it. She could have scrubbed behind my ears three times a day, and I would not have minded a minute of it. We loved her so very much and she is the one person from whom I remember receiving spontaneous demonstrations of love and cuddles.

I was a little less sure of my granddad. I could not remember his adoration of me as a baby, but I came to learn that he did love me dearly. He was the only person who ever tried to discourage me from biting my fingernails, which were always chewed down to the quick. He never succeeded in discouraging this awful habit, but neither did he ever give up trying. Could I have felt close enough to tell him my awful secret? I knew it was a secret, Daddy had told me so. Daddy had also told me that nobody else would understand that we had a very special relationship, and that he loved me very much. And I believed it was a special relationship; I wanted to please him, to make him love me more. What I could not know was that I did not need more of his kind of love. I needed a different kind of love, a real love, a giving, unselfish love; the love that every little girl deserves from her father.

Our family holidays consisted of day trips – sometimes with friends – out to the many seaside resorts along the North Kent coast. Some years, perhaps when money was less tight, my father would buy an old car just for the summer, selling it again in the autumn, and we would all pile in; the boot filled with our bags of swimming costumes and towels, picnic lunch, bats, balls and kites; though the journey would be governed by my father's need to visit the pub twice a day. If we had no car, then we would all troop to the local station and take the train. These were balmy days. Beautiful beaches; wide, long empty stretches of sand where we could run and run, arms open to the wind, down to the sea where we would splash and swim, rain or shine.

THE BEACH

Sandcastles built
Moats filled and imaginary cannons fired
Towers crushed
Enemy defeated
And tunnels collapsed
Buckets and spades left to one side
Used and discarded

Kites soaring high
Homemade with wooden sticks
Bound together
Pieces of cloth and odd bits of string
Paper bows fluttering
Legs pounding across the wide beach
Splashing through warm puddles
Seaweed, and salt water
Left by the receding tide

Cricket played won and lost
Both sides out
Who will run now
Across the sand to catch the ball?
Rolling forever
Towards the distant sea

The tide turns, sea rushing in
Cold and shivering in the late afternoon
Four children search for a new diversion

Away from the beach
Up across the dunes is a track
Narrow, wheel marked
Leading up a slope to a dilapidated wooden shed
Doors hanging loose, they peep inside

An old car chassis
Cross piece and four wheels
Two shabby and twisted seats
Stuffing, torn leather and rusty springs
And a steering wheel on a long metal column
Still connected
Tested
Still working

Boys climb aboard
Little girl less sure
Come on don't be a sissy

Open the doors wide
Push, harder
The vehicle starts slowly
Leaving the confines of its garage
Creaking, groaning at this unusual effort

Then it runs
Like the four children
Elated to be out and free
Gaining speed as it rolls down the track
Children shrieking with joy
Faster and faster

No brakes
The end of the track approaching fast
Last minute twist of the wheel and the old car jumps
Rumbles over the dune to a sudden halt
Wheels embedded in the soft, deep sand
Laughter subsides
Four pairs of hands
Grabbing, turning, pushing, pulling
The vehicle slowly dragged backwards up the slope

Again
Yes, again

Once more the thrill and excitement
Squeals and screams of delight

Overheard above the wind
And shouts of joy
Another shout
"What do you think you are doing?"

This time the journey
Back up the slope is filled
Not with anticipated excitement of the next run
But fear of chastisement

The owner?
A big, dark, overpowering man
Stares angrily at the four
As they approach with his property

Four faces turned down
Looking at the dusty track
Eight red cheeks
Waiting for the sword to fall

"Sorry mister
We didn't think"

"No you didn't
Did you?
Why not ask first?"

The expected anger not materialising
A slow grin spreads across the man's face
Go on – one more go then!

Occasionally we would visit the large open-air swimming pool in Gillingham. Unusually it was a circular pool. At one side was a concrete diving platform, and at the deep end a chute, like a children's slide, stopped just short of the water. The changing rooms were wooden, yellow painted blocks around the pool; men's and boy's around one side and women's and girl's the other. It was an extremely popular venue, but a very intimidating place for me, so crowded, the changing rooms chilly even in summer; very noisy, echoing with the sound of children screaming, and changing room doors constantly banging loudly. I hated taking my clothes off in such a public place, and would change as quickly as I could, hidden in my small cubicle, perpetually in fear of someone pushing their way in. Children can be cruel and I was often taunted about my skinny legs and arms. But my naked body represented something bad that was happening in my life. I was ashamed of it.

Even here, having survived my fears in the changing rooms, I was not free of my father's control. He insisted on teaching me to dive and to slide down the chute, an activity normally reserved for older, more confident children. He appeared to have a need to push me constantly to be better than other children of my age. I stood on the diving block, shaking, fearful, but listening to his instructions carefully, desperate to please. After some brief explanation, in I went, but I forgot to curve my hands and arms upward and kept on heading straight down. My head hit the bottom of the pool, and I can remember a dull clunk, like a muffled clanger in a bell, reverberating through my head and at the same time being struck by nausea. I think I was almost knocked unconscious, and for what seemed an age I was unable to determine which way the surface was. This was not fun. This was torture. I did not want to learn to dive. I wanted nothing more than to be left to play in the shallow end of the pool with my little brother. But I was incapable of telling my father this. Just as I was incapable of telling him that I did not like what we did in bed. I believed that my receipt of his love depended on me doing just as he wished, throughout every

51

aspect of my life. The power that he held over me was utterly complete. There was nothing I would refuse him.

In the winter months we would be taken to an indoor pool, closer to home, built originally as part of a new scout complex. I can remember being taken on my own, expressly to learn breaststroke, being told that I was now too old to use the doggy paddle.

Swimming Lesson

Inside pool
Noise echoing around the sweaty walls
Green, cold water

She makes an effort
Struggling in water
Out of her depth
Breaststroke
Not easy
For a child
Who doesn't want to
Swim

Who'd rather be
Playing
In shallow water
On her own

He supports her
One arm under her tummy

The other plays around her thighs
Near the top of
Her legs

Fingering the edge of her costume
Around the edge of her thigh
Suddenly intruding
Pushing into her

She wriggles
Kicks harder
Arms flailing
Gasping for breath

Hot, flushing
Even in the cold water
Shame
Urging her forward
Trying to escape
This feeling
Of very public
Humiliation

She hates them
Swimming lessons

CHAPTER 7

At the farthest end of the estate, the land was still open to fields and woods, where we would all roam, and find much to occupy our time. In spring the ground was a carpet of bluebells and we would come home with armfuls of them to put into vases or milk bottles. With the longer days we would venture deep into the woods, searching for adders or making rope swings from the overhanging tree branches. Sometimes we would walk for miles and finish up on the banks of the River Medway rummaging amongst the old wrecks, which lay in the stinking mud at the side of the river at low tide. In the autumn, evenings closing in, we would return home with bucketfuls of blackberries, picked from the bushes that lined the tracks that we walked. We were happiest out of the house, away from the tense atmosphere, and the fear of putting a foot wrong: apart from one incident we suffered no major mishaps or accidents.

Sunday afternoons, weather permitting, we were always 'locked out' until teatime, whether we wanted to be out or not. I don't think I had any understanding of deeper motives for my parent's wish to be alone; I just accepted what I was told, that they were tired and wanted a sleep. How would I have felt, had I made the connection that they may have been in bed together for sex? My relationship with my father was not sexual, not in the concept of the desire that is the normal precursor to sex in an adult relationship. I was a child, and not capable of understanding the depths of adult human desire, or of the compelling and utter need to possess that a sexual encounter can bring. Our sex was just a physical part of the relationship between father and daughter, albeit a part I disliked. So I doubt there would have been the emotions of jealousy and hatred, as there would be between two adult women upon discovering that they were sharing one man.

A high brick wall rounded the corner at the top of our road. The older children of the neighbourhood would run along this wall, balancing precariously, until they reached the far end where the street level came up to meet it on the short hill at the top of Windward Road. I can remember looking up in admiration at the older girls who were able to do this long before I could. Summer's evening would find large groups of children hanging around this walled area, chatting and generally fooling around. You knew you had 'arrived' when you were finally able to 'run the wall'. In the field across the road from the hill, at the far end of the wall, was another popular gathering place. An old block built hut, inset into the ground a little like a bomb shelter it had an open doorway and one small open window. This window represented another challenge to a growing child. By standing on the windowsill, if you were tall and brave enough, you could climb out and on to the roof of the hut. Late one afternoon, I was playing with two or three other children in and around the hut. I was alone inside the hut, the other children outside, when a man appeared in the doorway. He blocked my exit, and as I approached to try and leave he bent down on his knees and put his hand into my knickers. He touched and squeezed and I did nothing but stand there allowing him to assault me. Why did I not call out? Was it my conditioning, or would a 'normal' child have reacted in the same way? Standing there, patiently waiting for him to finish, I heard my mother's voice call from the edge of the field for us to come home for tea. The man stood up and ran off, past my mother and down into the road below where we lived. I ran to my mother, and recall her asking me accusingly, "What was that man doing to you?" I felt that I had done something wrong, knew she was angry. Her reaction was not to caress me and encourage me gently into telling what happened, but to demand an answer. Did she know instinctively that something was wrong – the other children must have seen something because I remember them asking me in school about the man who put his hand in my knickers – or did she guess from his guilty running away? The police were called, and I gave them a description but to my knowledge he was never found. I was excited by all the attention it gave me, sitting later on the lap of the kindly policewoman. I know that Mr Collins – the man who had held me whilst my brother was thrashed – was in the room because he was quite shocked when, asked what the man looked like, my reply was, "Well, a bit like Mr. Collins!" I have no idea how my father felt about this incident, but I wonder if he must have been terrified when the policewoman was questioning me, that I would bring up our relationship. The severity of what had happened did not strike me. After all it was nothing out of the ordinary for me, except that for the first time, it was another man, not my father.

The hut was subsequently destroyed and a block of shops built on the far side of the field. On dark winter's evenings my father would send me to these shops for cigarettes. I can recall being almost paralysed with fear on reaching the top of our road, facing the dark, open space that I must cross before reaching the safety of the brightly lit shops in the distance. Convinced that something was waiting to jump out on me, I would take a deep breath and then almost fly across the field to the shops, and then the same again coming back with his cigarettes. My father's work van was parked outside our house, but he insisted I walked to the shop, making the excuse that if he was caught using it for private errands he would lose his job. I cannot believe that it did not occur to him that it might be safer for him to walk to the shop, or that I may be just a little nervous of crossing the field alone – the field where I had been assaulted. His cruelty was usually reserved for my brothers.

In the next pair of semi-detached houses lived another Jackie, a girl who was a year older than me. Having more in common with her than I did with the boys on the other side, we developed a friendship, probably the strongest of my early childhood. Jackie and I often played together, girls' games of skipping, ball games and make believe. Jackie was often complaining that she did not feel well, or refused to skip because she had a sprained ankle, but she was happy to watch me. She was not a dominant character, and though her lack of enthusiasm often frustrated me, I was comfortable around her, even able to lead the way and make the rules, which was an unusual position for me to be in. I think this is why I was attracted to her and was able to enjoy her friendship. Perhaps also, in some way that I was not able to detect, she needed me as a friend as much as I needed her.

My father, desiring control even over my games with a friend would often interrupt our play to set us spelling tests. I almost always did better than she, despite her slight age advantage, and I think in some way it gave him a perverse pleasure to prove that something he had was better than the bloke's next door. But then I knew other ways to please him; I did not have to be good at spelling.

FIRST KISS

That's it
There
Yes, just there
Hold firmly
Right down
Then up
Yes, now kiss
The top
Lick
Oh God
You beautiful, clever little girl
Daddy's clever little girl
Now, in your mouth
Yes,
Yes you can
Gently
Suck
Oh God
Ahh…

Oh Daddy, Daddy!
I'm sorry Daddy
I'm sorry
I'm so sorry
I've hurt you

Hot tears flow fast from her eyes
Hot torrent of creamy milk flowing from his body

The milk of human kindness?

CHAPTER 8

Passing the 11 plus examination was quite an achievement. Only 5 pupils – three boys and two girls – out of a year of 166 were successful in that year: 1959. I elected to go to Chatham Grammar School for girls; although much farther away, it was preferable to Rochester, which had a reputation for being rather exclusive. My parents were proud of my success, and involved me in the choice of school. Though I remember my father was keen for me to go to the technical school, I wanted to go to grammar school which was, after all, the point of passing the 11 plus. In the event I think this was probably a crucial decision that proved to be the first step in getting me out of my father's clutches, though at the time I did not know it. My mother was worried about how they would pay for the uniform, which had to be purchased through a very smart shop in town, the list of items required being very long and specific. So during the following few months she took an evening job in the local paper factory, hard manual work, to save money for my new uniform. This was one sacrifice that she did make for me, and for which I am still grateful.

It was unusual for a girl from my background to go to grammar school; most of my contemporaries went on to the local secondary modern school and left at fifteen or sixteen to start work in local shops and factories. Nervous and shy, being dropped in amongst six hundred well brought up, well spoken and relatively wealthy young ladies took a great deal of adjustment on my part. However, I hung in, fading into the background as always, keeping my nose down and working hard. My results were not as spectacular as before of course. I was up against la crème de la crème of the Medway Towns, and although I found this very hard to understand, I kept working hard and managed passable results. My exercise books were all very neat, and any red crosses on them left me distraught. Consequently I would spend hours doing my homework, striving for the impossible – perfect answers to every question.

Once introduced to algebra I began to love the magic of mathematics. The maths teacher, Mrs Fennell, was very strict and exacting in her lessons, but she seemed to take a liking to me, realising that she had a keen pupil. Her encouragement and approval proved to be a strong force in my years at grammar school. I looked forward to her lessons, thriving on my success in this subject, feeling for the first time in my life that I was being praised for something which I not only enjoyed taking part in, but which I appeared to be good at. I sensed a softness in her, a characteristic that she strived to keep hidden in the classroom environment. I look upon her now as another of the stepping-stones in my childhood that carried me through the swirling torrent of my life, throwing a lifeline and preventing me from falling into an emotional morass from which I would never be able to escape.

At around this time I had become friendly with a rather large and bossy but likeable girl called Janet, who lived in our road for a short period. Her family were staunch Catholics, and Janet had introduced me to a Friday club held in a small hut behind the local Catholic Church. It was through this club that another supportive presence came into my life. Father Kirby, a small Irishman who had instigated the club, was there almost every week, encouraging, chatting, listening to our crazy music, playing ping-pong and indulging us in whatever games or conversations we wanted. I found in him a male adult presence that was loving, comforting and safe, where I could test the expression of my own opinions and wishes without fear of reprisal. I became extremely fond of him, with the consequence that when he was moved back to Ireland, and the club had to close, a large hole was left in my life.

One of my greatest delights whilst at grammar school was to visit my grandmother after school, for a cup of coffee. Her house was only about ¾ mile from the school, and she always had the kettle on, and homemade cakes out ready for me. I loved that little old lady with all my heart. I can still smell her, and feel her around me when I conjure up memories of my times spent with her. Her home was my shelter from the storm. Those precious hours spent with her, delaying the time when I must return home, were a constant source of annoyance to my father. When I eventually arrived home, if it was later than the anticipated time from the 3.55pm bus, his displeasure would become evident in his demand to know why I was not at home on time and where I had been. His need to check my every move was so overriding that he would even admit to driving past the school bus stop to check that I was in the queue at 3.50pm. He must have lived in fear that I would confide in her about our 'special relationship'.

A Snapshot of Childhood

The school bell rings
Resounding in the corridor outside the classroom
Signifying the end of the final lesson
Algebra, calculus
Dealing with unknown quantities
Difficult for some

Mrs Fennell – the archetypal, stern, no nonsense mistress of
Class 4A
Cut off in mid sentence
Chalk poised over an algebraic problem
Blackboard masked with the mysteries of quadratic equations –
Turns to look at the group of girls
Some, a small proportion, sitting upright at their desks
Others, lolling back in their chairs, arms folded
And one or two lying spread across the desk, legs twined
around the chair legs

A look of resignation on her face
But, tinged with relief, a tiny smile flickers at the corner of her
mouth
For the bell's ring holds the same message for her
A whole half-day off school

From the obedient, silent attention of fifteen pairs of eyes
Struggling to follow the logic of the myriad of symbols and
mathematical signs
The classroom erupts into the unruly, thumping noise
Of books being swept unceremoniously from desktops into
satchels
Pencils and rulers being crammed into pencil cases
Chairs scraping with a tooth edge sound as they are pushed
back and away from the desks
All fifteen girls suddenly chattering with the excitement of
plans and projects

Which a free afternoon will bring
Rushing to pack up and leave
The physical and mental confines of the classroom
To make for the freedom that exists beyond the school gates

All, that is, except one

She stands alone amongst the chattering group
Her books not swept from the desk
In the eager rush to abandon the problems of calculus for
more pleasurable pursuits
But lifted – each one with a heavy hand –
And packed slowly, meticulously into her school bag
To an outside observer it would appear that she was
Unwilling
To finish the lesson and leave
To rush on to some new assignation

Does the teacher notice?
If she does, she says nothing
She does not ask if there is a problem
Maybe too engrossed in her own plans for the half day release
Or maybe, this quiet child
Just does not command attention, as her noisy companions do

Her deep set eyes – hooded from closer inspection
Lest they reveal her soul
Her innermost thoughts of self-loathing –
Flicker over her classmates
Was there not one who would say
"What are you doing this afternoon?
Why not come home with me?
Walk through the woods and pick the bluebells
Sit in the branches of trees and dream of boyfriends to come
Go home for tea – sandwiches, jelly and ice cream, and home-
made cake –
Listen to our favourite pop records"

Hope against hope
For she knows it will not happen
Standing amongst
But separate from,
The crowd
An oddity
Ugly
Unattractive
And knowing that because of this
She will never be welcomed into their circle.

She watches them drift homeward in twos and threes
Whispering the secrets that teenage girls alone can share
Resigned and with a heavy heart
She waits alone in the queue outside the school
For the bus which will take her
Home
A journey filled with a strange mixture of dread and desperate
hope
What will she find?
What awaits her at journey's end?
She knows the answer
But still
Wishes it were not true

Last stop before the end of the line
She leaves the bus
Starting the long walk to the house at the other end of the
daily journey
A walk during which she prays fervently
If there is a God
If You are really there
Listen to my cries for help
And change the pattern

But He does not hear
Or is not there

Her heart sinks, despair and hopelessness rushing in as she
rounds the corner
And sees the all too familiar vehicle
Parked outside the house
Signifying the reality of her free afternoon
The horrors awaiting inside the house
Why can she not stop now?
Walk away
Go anywhere
Anywhere but through that door
Is she so feeble?
So unable to make her own choices
To say "No"
But it is not a question of strength or courage
The pattern is set
Long ago laid down on the blank tape of her mind

There is no such thing as refusal
His power over her is omnipotent
Unquestionable

She enters the house through the back door
Quietly
Almost creeping
Puts down her school bag
And opens her books upon the dining room table
Not stopping for the pleasure of a drink and a biscuit
Immediately trying to convey a message
I have to work this afternoon
I must get on
But he ignores her silent plea
Takes her by the hand and leads her up the stairs

This is our secret
Mummy would not understand
So don't tell her
Just between us
Our special secret

Mummy!
Mummy will be home from work soon
Her brothers home from school

She dresses
Returns to the kitchen
Prepares the supper
Sets the table in the dining room
All these tasks carried out in silence
While she remains
Uncommunicative
Deep in her own thoughts

"Is that child in one of her moods again?"

After the meal the usual arguments over who will wash
And who will dry the dishes
Her mother gets out the ironing board
Her father reading the paper
Her brothers squabbling over a card game
She starts her homework
And slides back into the normality of family life.

Until the next time

CHAPTER 9

It was soon after I started at grammar school that I met up with yet another Jackie who used the same bus route to go to our school, getting on two stops after me each morning. Jackie and I very soon became firm and fast friends. She was very tall, 5ft 8", and slim, with a slight curvature of her upper spine for which she later had to take deportment lessons to correct her stature. Her shoulder-length, jet-black hair would grow a thin silver streak through the front section every so often, and we often mused about how this came about. She was a quiet girl and like me did not have many friends. For me, already labelled at home as a moody child, lacking in confidence and having no self esteem, it was impossible to push my way into the noisy, chatty groups of girls around the playground, or in the changing rooms. So Jackie was a gift beyond price – someone who seemed to like me, and wanted to be my friend.

It was the early sixties. I fell in love with the Beatles, and Jackie with Elvis. She was besotted with him and imagined all sorts of scenarios where she would meet him and they would fall in love. Eventually she started to write her stories down, and we would while away the time on our bus journey to school each morning reading what she had written the night before. I lost count of how many notebooks she must have used over the many months that the stories developed, but they were full of unrequited teenage passion. I was more practical in my devotion to the Beatles and just enjoyed listening and dancing to the music, though I must confess I had a passion for George Harrison. The magic of the unknown male-female relationships that Jackie wrote about were neither tantalising nor mysterious for me. Her writing was her growing up, her experiencing by proxy what she had not yet known, but what she knew was waiting for her when she became a woman. I had been denied the sweetness of that time when a young woman begins to lose innocence, when she delights in imagining what it would be like to be held by a man for the first time.

NEW TOY

The man's body
Arches over the tiny one below
Looming, threatening
Erect
And powerful

Two shadowy figures
Like a Japanese lantern show
In a macabre dance
They merge
The gap between them narrowing

Open your legs
Further

Pushing against the tiny opening
Harder
A gasp of frustration
You're still too small

It hurts
Daddy

I'm sorry
Daddy

The man's body
Lowering and lying
Next to
The child's

I'll give you something
A special toy
You can practice with it

Stepping away from the bed
Reaching into the back of a cupboard
Look, here it is
This is where it lives

Use it,
Often
And then you'll soon be ready
For the real thing

She holds the new toy
In her hand
Black
Shiny exterior
Long
Tapering

She looks at it
Unable to speak
Express what she feels
Sick
Dread
Revulsion

Knowing that she cannot
Of her own volition
Take it
From the cupboard

This black shiny toy

And push it
Into her body

An act to perform
In her bedroom
Alone
Hidden

Because
This is
Repulsive
Shameful
Dirty

And so will she be

Jackie and I built our own little world, growing together from gawky teenagers into young women, experimenting with clothes, make up and hair, and becoming interested in boys, a much discussed topic in the junior common room. We became very close, almost like sisters. Our time together very soon graduated from the school bus to Saturday morning shopping when we would meet at her house and travel into town, dressed to kill. Mooching around the teenage clothes shops, where in those days you could buy a mini skirt for 14 shillings, and a top for 5 shillings; browsing through stacks of E.P.s and 45s in the record shops, we were in our element. No outing was complete until we had taken our cappuccino coffee at Marco's coffee shop in the centre of Chatham High Street. This idyllic arrangement came to an end when my Christmas Saturday job in the large toyshop in town was offered to me as a year-round job. I had to take it, as it was my only source of income. A day's wage, 19s 6p, would buy clothes, tights and make-up.

I lived in two worlds during these early teen years although there was always an overlap of the two; the moodiness and anxiety of the home child spilling over into school life, teachers remarking in reports that "she must not let anxiety prevent her from achieving more"; "she needs to gain more confidence"; "she is a very quiet child". But at school, or with Jackie, I could at least try to discover who I was – I could make choices about what I would do, and when, and how. As the years passed we became inseparable; neither of us dominating characters, we easily adapted to each other's needs, so many of which were the same. I cannot recall a single argument with Jackie – we didn't even fancy the same boys. Yes I did fancy boys and I cannot explain why, when even to me it would seem that I should hate all things to do with men. But I think it is all to do with the building of two separate worlds – two lives, like a female Jekyll and Hyde, one that lived in the normal world of school and teenage dreams, and the other – hidden, dark and unlovable, dealing with the hellish existence that was my home life.

PICTURES

I've got something to show you
A book
You like books
Don't you?

Stay there
In bed
Only up here, top shelf
Wardrobe
At the back

Yes here it is

See
Look at them
What they're doing

Obediently
She looks
Sees
What they are doing

In the photo
Black and white
But clear
Shockingly clear

A woman
On all fours
Like a dog

One man
Kneeling at her head
Holding her hair

Her mouth
Open and full

Another man
Kneeling behind her
His hands clutching
The flesh of her bottom

The threesome
Caught
Still life
Yet the picture imparting movement

What do you think?

What does she think!
She can't think

Only look
Words not forming
Even in her mind

Only look
Must look
He tells her it's nice
He tells her
When you are a little bit bigger you will be able to do that

What does she think?

She doesn't want to
Think
Or do it
Even when she is older
Will she?

It is now recognised that victims of childhood sexual abuse are at a high risk of re-victimisation; of being raped, or experiencing sexual harassment. I wonder at what stage in the victim's life this increased risk begins to take effect. Why was I the little girl out of our group of friends who was assaulted in the hut in the field? I recall a further incident when I was set upon by a group of boys. The bus journey on a Friday evening from the grammar school in Gillingham to home could take upward of two hours, and so on summer days we would often walk. One Friday I was walking alone along a path across a local park, when a group of boys surrounded me, jostling against me, and pulled my bag from my shoulder. Perhaps emboldened by my fear, one in particular grabbed me, pulled me down to the ground, and rolled down the nearby bank clutching me to him. We finished in the ditch at the bottom with him laying on top of me, hands gripping my shoulders, wild eyes staring into mine. Frozen with fear, awaiting his next move, I could not even try to push him off. Had he planned his attack? Or had the matter spiralled ahead of any initial idea of a bit of harmless fun, the instant that his male instincts sensed my female fear, as I lay beneath him? Was he now as frightened as I, realisation dawning on him of the awful power that had suddenly been handed to him. A momentous moment became an age as we both waited for his decision. He pushed himself up, kicked me, not hard, and then walked away rejoining his friends who were waiting at the top of the bank, watching expectantly perhaps for some new experience. I lay there, shaking, waited until the sound of their voices disappeared into the distance. And then tidying my clothes, and retrieving my bag I continued my journey home. I was to be attacked twice more in the succeeding years, neither resulting in serious harm, but both shocking and frightening events for me. There must be a demeanour or body language that portrays the victim, a label that can be seen and read, enticing a would-be perpetrator.

"Here I am, an easy target." Yet another bequest from the abuser to his victim.

CHAPTER 10

Try to fathom the complexities of the mind of a child struggling to deal with the twisted relationship, as yet unrecognised as abusive, that she had with her father. The first man in her life, whose role was to love, guide, teach and protect. The love, guidance, and teaching were there, but for self-gratification. There was protection, but shown as obsessive control, preventing normal relationships with other people, male and female. And the growing child was unaware that this was a destructive love, wrongful love; believing that it was a normal part of childhood, but like visits to the dentist, a part that had to be endured not enjoyed.

I was growing older, but my body was still that of a young girl. My breasts had barely begun to develop, and my periods had not started. Emotionally I was ready to begin experimenting with being a woman. My father used me as a woman, but he wanted me to remain a little girl. Why? What is the perverted reasoning that causes this need in a man. Surely my skinny little body could not have aroused a natural male desire? Every effort that the teenage girl made to become a woman was destroyed or dismissed, and often publicly. The pudding bowl hair cut, arranged without consultation, which made me look like a six year old, not able to back comb or spray into any of the latest styles. The sarcastic comments made in the presence of other adults about my attempts at eye make-up. The crushing and destructive effect of cruel comments about the waste of money spent on my first bra. Not in fact, bought by my mother, but by an older cousin who had asked me to be bridesmaid at her wedding.

His cruel, and yet almost desperate, attempts at keeping me as his little girl were doomed to failure. He could overpower the child, but he stood no chance against Mother Nature. His time was running out, and unbeknown to me, my burgeoning womanhood would be the wellspring of my fight back to regain control over my life. Deep within the young woman was the fighting spirit that had tried to save her brother from a thrashing, a spirit that rebelled at the sign of any injustice. Perhaps the subliminal effects of a grammar school education where we were taught to think for ourselves, had encouraged it, or maybe it was just a stubborn trait that I had inherited, but that little spark in me was about to flare and engulf us both.

I had reached the age of fifteen and still my periods had not started. My mother, concerned, took me to the doctor, because at the time I was having dizzy spells. He could not give any reason, but prescribed an iron tonic. Whether this triggered the process or not, I don't know, but around nine months later I had my first period. The little girl had grown up, and though she did not yet realise it, everything would now change.

Once my periods began, my father no longer wanted me in his bed. Was this revulsion, or was it because I was now a young woman and if he persisted, I could become pregnant? His sexual demands stopped, but his need to control me did not.

The precarious balance of our relationship tipped. Suddenly the love was no longer on offer. Wrong love is better than no love, especially when the love is withdrawn at a time of great change, when the fledgling woman is struggling to become a beautiful bird. Instead of gentle encouragement to experiment and fly the nest, there was constriction, denial, disgust and rejection.

I began to question his dominance over my every move at home, where life gradually became more intolerable. His efforts at control caused explosive rows within the family. My mother wanted a quiet life. What switch had been thrown, and why then, why had the child accepted all the years of abuse, and yet now fought this authority?

For whatever reason, the worm had turned. My friend was not told when to bath, not ridiculed at her use of hair spray, or eye make-up, or high heels so I could and did publicly reject these controls. The other control was different, not up for discussion; always told, "This is our special little secret – no-one else would understand." It remained buried deep inside, the shame and guilt all part of my self image, biding its time, waiting for the right moment to erupt – and destroy everything in its path, even its host, many years hence.

It was through the Friday club that I had my first experience of teenage love. Ralph was handsome and rode a motorbike, and would arrive at the club in his black leathers, helmet tucked under his arm. Convinced that I was unattractive and could never form any relationship with him, I was unable to push myself or offer any hint of encouragement for fear of rejection, but we would always look at each other with a strange deep longing. The effect that he had on me was almost electric, as Jackie remarked. One evening we were standing at the far end of the clubroom with our backs to the door. Someone came in and I started to shake, knowing it was him without seeing him. I looked and longed from afar whilst he appeared to be surrounded by girl friends, but I never gave up hope. I later learned from a mutual friend that he had been waiting for me to make the first move.

I can remember a particular incident after the enforced haircut when my father insisted that I go to the local shops to fetch something for him. The trip to the shop meant that I had to pass Ralph's house; Ralph the boy for whom I had waited so patiently to notice me. I was petrified that he would see how awful I looked. I recall standing at the top of the stairs looking down at my father, refusing to go; he standing at the bottom, demanding I go now. Our wills clashing mid-air somewhere halfway up the staircase; clash of the Titans, a battle fought in the ether with weapons of the spirit. My mother stood beside him, looking up at me, pleading that I go as requested, anxious to avoid another pitched battle. The next thing I can remember is the back of my head banging on every step of the stair case on the way down to the bottom as he dragged me, feet first, to the front door and threw me out.

CHAPTER 11

Jackie and I were bound together academically as well as socially, and so it was almost a foregone conclusion that we would move on together to the sixth form, both taking pure and applied maths and physics A-levels. Through our trips to the Friday club she met a boy called Roy. They became an item and it was inevitable that she would start to spend more time with him than with me. But we had teamed up with another pair of girls at school: Lesley and Susan, and whilst Jackie and I remained the closest of friends at school, I was able to switch to Susan and Lesley for my Friday or Saturday night entertainment. Lesley was an absolute disaster zone; funny, bright, accident prone, devil-may-care, her every sentence punctuated with expletives. She was just what I needed to assist my efforts to break free from the smothering control of my father. Joining up with Lesley opened up my field of vision, and we ventured further afield for our weekend sorties; once getting into a precariously dangerous situation when, petrified of overrunning my father's strict curfew, we accepted a lift home from a couple of sailors. Asked where to, I gave my address as the first port of call, and whilst I had to contend with only one wandering hand in the front seat I could hear Lesley's voice from the rear punctuating the air with her favourite words, between sounds of rustling and tugging of clothes.

The second year of sixth form was very hard work. Finishing the syllabus, trying old papers, and revision took up much of our time, both at school and at home. Jackie and I still travelled back and forth most days, but occasionally Roy would pick her up on the bike. Weekends, they would often go out on the bike with another couple; the North Kent coast was not a long drive away, and it was a lovely way to spend a Sunday afternoon, at any time of the year. One Monday morning in early January 1966, a day that will remain indelibly printed on my mind, all of the upper sixth form were called into the common room. The headmistress and our form mistress came in, both looking very shaken, and we nudged each other, wondering what on earth they were about to say. The headmistress stepped forward and began haltingly: "I am very sorry to tell you that yesterday evening, at around 5.00pm Jackie Miles was killed in a motorbike accident…" My knees buckled and the two girls either side caught me as I slipped to the floor. I was taken, devastated, to the headmistress' room, where she expressed her deep sorrow that I had heard so publicly. She had assumed that as we were so close I would have either been with Jackie, or at least known about her death. I was taken home, and I remember walking into the kitchen and seeing my mum standing at the cooker – "Oh mum – Jackie's dead." She took me in her arms, both of us crying uncontrollably. My alter ego, my soul mate, the one person who had unknowingly carried me through my tortuous and tempestuous teenage years had gone, leaving me to carry on alone.

A-levels loomed, and the maths teacher, still Mrs Fennell, pushed me hard, expecting me to achieve 'A' grades. Maybe she thought it would divert my thoughts from the terrible loss of a close friend and confidant. Other members of staff were also unable to speak their words of comfort, but in their looks showed sympathy. The funeral was a desperately sad affair, particularly as Roy died three days after the crash, and they were buried together. Both sets of parents were devastated, but the pain that Jackie's father bore was possibly the worst. From him she had inherited her black hair, and height, and her temperament. The week before the crash, she and he had argued badly over some silly issue, and neither had made an effort to apologise or make up. His pain was terrible to see, and though I did not keep in touch with her parents – her mother could not bear to see me for the reminder of the lovely daughter she had lost – I did hear that he became very unwell and soon afterwards they moved away.

The Christmas before the accident our sixth form had shared a disco with the boys at the local boys grammar school, and I had met a boy called Tony. He was quite good looking, but spoiled by his doting parents, and had a very high opinion of himself and his abilities. He and I had started dating: I do not know what the initial attraction was, but after Jackie's death I think I switched my devotions to him as the only person available and interested. Dating was a very difficult path for me to tread and, as it turned out, also for my boyfriend. I had never brought a boy home, had never had a steady boyfriend anyway, and would only ever agree to meet boys at dances or the cinema, and then find my own way home. In this respect I was therefore relatively inexperienced dealing with boys, even at age eighteen. Because Tony came to mean something to me – we even discussed getting engaged before he went to university – I invited him home to meet my parents. I should have known better – even before he met him, my father was not going to like him, particularly since he drove a Lambretta scooter, which in my parents' eyes was no different to a motorbike. I remember arriving home one night after we had taken a small tumble from the scooter on a tight corner in the freezing snow, my tights torn and my knees bleeding badly. Luckily my mother was at home alone, and whilst I tried to creep upstairs before she could see the state that I was in, she heard me and came up. "What have you done? You have been on that boy's bike," she accused angrily. Tony was a slow steady driver, and I only travelled on the back of his bike infrequently, but I could understand her anxiety after what had happened to Jackie.

So, I had decided to introduce Tony to my parents. He arrived and I opened the door. Before I could warn him, he strode boldly up the narrow hallway, heading for the kitchen, and did not see the newly pasted strip of wallpaper that my father had laid out on the hall floor prior to sticking to the wall. The paper wrapped itself around his feet and legs, getting him more entangled as he tried vainly to free himself. I wanted to laugh, and so I think did my mother, but we did not dare. My father exploded, and called the poor boy every name he could think of. Our love survived, but I did not invite him home again, though I don't think wild horses could have dragged him back.

I took my A-levels in May/June. I had wanted to go to university, but my father, either eager to get another source of income into the house, or still trying to control my life, had put a stop to my thoughts of further education. The only person who had encouraged me to dream that I could read maths at university was Mrs Fennell. Unbeknown to me my father visited the headmistress and convinced her that I was not confident enough to cope with the demands of a degree. Whether she agreed or not, I was never consulted. However, my darling grandfather stepped in to help, suggesting that I join the Civil Service. He was excited by the idea that at eighteen, and with my qualifications, I could walk straight into the level that had taken him twenty years to reach. He convinced me to try, and when I went for the interview in London, they advised me that with my maths I could become a computer programmer. So I took a barrage of aptitude tests, and waited.

Rochester boasted a castle; not a grand affair like Warwick or Windsor, but situated at the end of the old High Street behind the cathedral and on the banks of the river Medway it was a popular venue. That summer the castle was hosting a musical festival finishing with a firework display at ten o'clock, and as Tony and I were going I asked my father if we could stay until the fireworks finished. The answer was "No," and as usual an argument ensued. I left feeling that I could maybe stretch it to 10.15, and at least see the start of the display. We arrived back at the house just after 10.15. Although the lights were on in my parents' bedroom, both front and rear doors were locked. I had never been given a house-key so I knocked on the front door, but to no avail. Tony hovered around unsure of what to do. We decided that he would drop me off at my grandparents' as it was on his way home. Arriving a little before 10.45pm I knocked on the door, somewhat nervous of their reaction. It was almost as if they were expecting me – they could not have been because they had no telephone – and of course I could stay the night.

Since leaving school, and whilst waiting for my job application results, I had been working in the same office as my mother, above a department store owned and run by a local family in Rochester High Street. The morning after the firework fiasco, tired of my father's continuous unfair control in my life, I asked my grandparents if I could move in with them. They agreed, though were a little concerned about how my mother would take it. She did find it very hard, especially as she was seeing me at work every day, and was often tearful in my presence. I have no idea how my father reacted or what his thoughts were. Once again though, I wonder how fearful he was of my finding a confidant in one of my grandparents. I guess my mother and younger brothers had to deal with any furious outbursts that may have been the result of my actions. Though I felt a little guilty at my mother's sadness, I was happier than I could ever remember being. But my happiness was still subject to the vagaries of others' behaviour. Many people seem willing to make crucial judgements on a given situation without having any idea of the reasons behind the problem, or any full understanding of the consequence of their input. My mother's friends at work kept talking to me, slowly drip feeding my guilt complex and convincing me that I was "breaking your mother's heart", that "your dad would change", and "things will be different". Eventually I caved in and I moved back home. My mother was happier, but otherwise nothing changed.

I passed the examination for the Civil Service, and so in September 1966 I started training as a computer programmer, working in Aldgate East, near Cable Street, East London for the division of the Civil Service that was then known as GPO. Tony went down to Southampton University, and we remained in touch, with occasional visits by me to the campus, where a local lady gave me bed and breakfast.

I settled well into my new job and soon became friendly with another girl, Chris, a lively blonde from Warrington who shared a flat in West Kensington with two other girls; one from Sheffield and another from Liverpool. The winter passed in a haze of early morning trains, challenging new work, and occasional weekends in Southampton. I discovered a new world. London in the late '60s was an exciting place to be, and the parties, shops and young men beckoned. I soon came to realise that I no longer wanted even to remain tied to my one last link with my previous life – my boyfriend Tony. We spent a dreadful weekend when I went to see him to tell him it was all over. He did not take it at all well, so there was yet one more person adding to my guilt and my conviction that I was responsible for other people's happiness.

There was, however, one other link that remained firmly in place. The geographical distance was not enough to break the strings that attached me to my father. He called my office desk almost daily. Did he still need to prove that he had control over my life from sixty miles away? I hated those calls, in which he still insinuated that we had a special relationship. He would use the same tone of voice as he had when he had taken me into his bed, reminding me vividly of experiences that I would rather forget, bringing back guilt and shame. Embarrassment would flood over me, and I would be acutely aware of the office full of men around me, convincing myself that they would sense what was happening, would somehow know about our special relationship, and gain some perverse pleasure from this knowledge.

I started to stay over one or two nights and then even longer in the flat with Chris and the girls, and by Spring 1967 I had decided to leave home and move into the flat permanently. It would be cramped, but the rent could be shared five ways instead of four. The move bought with it a great sense of freedom.

The day that I left home was not a celebration of growing up, not a wonderful experience of proudly showing my parents my new flat and friends. I remember standing on the doorstep of the house in Leeward Road, under the canopy that my brother used to climb down. Beside me, in a new suitcase and a couple of carrier bags were my clothes, plus as many of the few treasured physical remains of eighteen years of life as I could carry. The emotional baggage was deeply tucked away, quietly waiting for the trigger that would bring it to life.

"Well, goodbye then."
"Yes goodbye."

And, carrying pretty much the sum of my life in my two hands, I walked the five miles to Rochester station alone.

PART 2: PHILIP

CHAPTER 12

Key in hand, I stood in front of the main doorway that was the entrance to my new home. Through this door, up the stairs on the right, and there it would be, my very own front door. My suitcase sat behind me on the shingle drive. Well girl, here you go again. My thoughts racing I hardly heard a voice behind me saying, "What do you want taken up first?"

As I came out of my reverie and looked over my shoulder toward the small furniture van parked in the driveway, my eyes met those of my husband, looking at me expectantly, waiting for me to change my mind. I knew I wouldn't. I had been through this process before, twenty-five years previously in 1967, when I left home, a young girl of nineteen.

My few belongings were soon safely offloaded, the empty rooms in the small apartment each containing a few packing boxes and a bare minimum of furniture. I offered them a cup of tea. They declined, and as I moved closer to kiss my husband goodbye, he whispered in my ear, "You'll be back."

So much had happened in those intervening years – marriage, three children, a successful business. For the most part the years had been happy. It was 1st November 1993, three weeks before what should have been a 25th wedding anniversary celebration. The clock on the time bomb ticking away in me during these last forty years had started its final countdown and I knew that the catalyst that had started this had been the birth of our daughter Katie in 1981.

I had met Philip, my future husband, soon after moving to London in 1967. Chris and I had decided to move out of the dingy basement flat on the busy Cromwell Road in West Kensington, into a smarter, greener part of the world. We passed many evenings after work closeted in a call box with the Evening Standard and a biro, finally being lucky enough to find a part share in a beautiful top floor apartment on the hill in Richmond; a vibrant town sporting boutiques, bistros, good pubs, a cinema and a lovely theatre on the green. We moved into the flat on Saturday 29th September 1967.

That first evening I was alone in the flat, but could tell from the music emanating from below that there must be a party in either the ground floor or basement flat. Sometime late in the evening came the sound of feet charging up the stairs to our entrance, followed by a banging on the door. Tentatively I opened it. Two girls and a boy stood there apologising, asking if they could use our loo, as there was a queue for the one downstairs. They asked me why I was sitting at home on my own, and when I explained that I had just moved in and did not really know anyone in the house, they would not leave until I agreed, reluctantly, to join the party. The boy was attractive, an air steward called Philip, and he and I chatted and danced for some time.

THE STRANGER

He came to her door unexpectedly
The strange young man
Sorry – can I use your loo?
Downstairs full
Too long to wait

Of course
Help yourself

Why not come down?
The party's in full swing
You'll enjoy
Come on, with me

Well, I don't know
Hesitant
Unsure of these new friends

Go on, I want you to
Well, if you're sure it's OK

Drinks in hand
Music loud, bodies moving
Dance?
Yes, please

You're gorgeous
I like you
I want you
Next time I see you
I don't care where or when
I will make love to you

Oh!
Fine

Er – Yes
Well, goodnight then

Days pass
She shops
Sainsbury's
Choosing vegetables
She feels eyes on her
Looking round, over her shoulder
He is there
Their eyes meet
Shock registers

Do they both remember his last words?
She does

At the checkout
A slow smile
Spreads across her face

It was at that same party that I met another Philip. I chatted to him and his friends, but did not find him immediately attractive, particularly as he was a little the worse for wear after a full evening's drinking following a successful rugby match. The following afternoon, Sunday, a telephone call came for me. I took the call somewhat bemused as there were very few people, if any, who would have known my new telephone number.

"Hello, it's Philip, remember, we met last night?"

"Oh – yes, Hello."

He asked me out that evening and I agreed to go, assuming that it was Philip the air steward. Imagine my shock when a few hours later I opened the door to Philip the now sober, but nevertheless unexpected, rugby player. A trip to the cinema was followed by a Chinese meal, over which we began to get to know each other. My feelings about him must have changed during the evening as the following Saturday found me at the rugby club fancy dress dance, wearing his rugby shirt as a dress and jock strap as a headband!

I grew to like him and was impressed with his strength, both physically and mentally. It wasn't the passionate love affair that every girl dreams of, but he cared for me, and treated me very well. He soon became the new rock in my life, filling the void that Jackie had left, and I clung to him dearly. I loved him. But I can recognise now that my love was born of a faulty perception that love was given as a condition of my subservience to the other's needs. I worked hard at keeping him in love with me, trying in every way I could to please him. I was unable to accept his love as a natural feeling in response to me as a person; to my looks, my character and my chemistry.

Philip had more than enough confidence for both of us; I did not need any of my own and was happy for him to take centre stage and make all the decisions, satisfying his need for a woman who would not endeavour to alter his life, and certainly not to run it.

CHAPTER 13

During our courtship I began to experience periods of deep depression. Not understanding why I was so tearful and low, I visited a doctor and, unquestioning, took the anti-depressant tablets that were readily given to me. Of course, they would not solve the problem, they could not 'cure' me but they helped to mask the symptoms, and I was able to function pretty normally, though I did have a great deal of time off work. It did cause some rocky moments in our relationship, because I became very nervous and somewhat jealous of other women, but Philip hung in there, I think because he already believed that I could be the girl for him.

I learned not to expect spontaneity or overt passion from Philip. Dependable, steady, loyal and protective; at that time in my life he was everything I needed, if not a match for my passionate nature. However, he did excel himself, and even my wildest dreams, with his proposal of marriage. In the summer of 1968 we decided to take a holiday together in France and Spain, and we set off in his small MGB sports car, packed to the hilt with all our needs for two weeks camping. Philip had decided that we should spend a day in Paris on our way through France, as I had never visited the city. He insisted that we take the lift right to the top of the Eiffel Tower and it was whilst we were standing there, looking out over the Bois du Boulogne that he asked me to marry him. My response was to burst into tears, overcome by this uncharacteristic show of romance.

We married the following November in 1968, giving our parents very short notice. The wedding was in Rochester, at St Justus' Church; a new church built since I had left the area, on spare land opposite the field where I had been assaulted as a little girl.

When I look now at the photograph of my father standing next to me outside the church, his arm looped through mine, I feel sick. How smug he looks, back in control, allowing me to go to another man, knowing our little secret, knowing that he knew me as intimately as Philip did. Philip was unaware that he was getting damaged goods. It would be several years before he became aware of the mess that I was in inside and even then would have no real appreciation of the seriousness of the problem.

The honeymoon was a brief three-day break in the rain in Bigbury on Sea, Devon, because Philip wanted to be home by Wednesday evening for rugby training. Home was the small post-war bungalow that his father had built for his growing family, in a quiet cul-de-sac in Staines, near the river Thames, and from where Philip ran his transport business.

Philip had insisted that I would give up work when we married, so two days before the wedding I had said goodbye to my boss and colleagues. My boss was a kindly man and I remember a tearful goodbye at the station after the farewell drinks party. I think I had begun to look upon him as a surrogate father – a father who was only ever kind to me.

I had fallen in line with Philip's decision that I should leave work without really thinking what I would do with my time, and so I found that first winter very long and lonely, with no friends in the area, and no real human contact all day. But I loved caring for our little bungalow – my grandmother had taught me how to clean and polish, hand wash and iron – and I took great pride in making it homely for us. I read a great many books, and I took some evening classes in cookery, which I thoroughly enjoyed, and which were very rewarding for both of us. However, in the spring of 1969 I told Philip that I needed something more to fill my life. As he did not want me to return to work, I asked if I could help with his paperwork, which in the main consisted of a pile of envelopes, notes and diaries laying in total confusion on the kitchen worktop. And so our business partnership began.

It was around this time that we became involved with another young couple whose lives were to become inextricably linked with ours. Mick was the same age as me and had started to work for Philip casually as a driver just before we married. Philip discovered that Mick did not in fact have a full licence and arranged for him to take a driving test. I had passed my own driving test a week before our wedding, and so it fell to me to drive Mick to the testing centre. This early working relationship was the beginning of a lifelong friendship that Mick and I have formed. His girlfriend, Dawn, was only fourteen at this time and officially still at school, and it would be many years yet before she and I began our deep and lifelong friendship. Life has a strange way of bringing people into your circle as players, people who you often take at face value and as just another cog in the wheel of your life, but whose true value and role does not become apparent until the wheel has travelled much further along the road. Dawn and Mick are two such people who have remained close to me throughout the unfolding story of my life. They know more than most the true depth of my descent into hell, and of my struggle back.

Time passed fairly uneventfully and though I had a difficult start to the relationship with my mother-in-law – Philip was the only boy amongst five children – we eventually managed an uneasy truce.

We had been married for a little under two years when Philip suggested that we should have a baby. I agreed without really understanding what it would mean and what a huge impact it would have on my life. Consequently our first child was soon conceived and was due sometime in mid June 1971. I did not go into labour spontaneously, and was induced at 10.00am on the 7th July. It became a marathon struggle for both of us, and a catalogue of disasters. Eventually, at around 9.00am the next morning my contractions ceased. Though drugged with Pethidine, I was nonetheless dimly aware that an atmosphere of panic had set in. Philip was ushered out, and the midwife went in search of a registrar. Adam was finally delivered by forceps, at 10.40am, looking very battered. It still amazes me that he arrived with nothing more than a bruise to his forehead and a slight scar below his right eye. I lay there watching the nurses tidy him up, feeling as though I had been turned inside out. But when I took him in my arms I immediately felt the most overwhelming love rushing through me for this tiny, bruised little being.

Being a worrier and perfectionist, I found the responsibility of looking after this new human being – my child – very onerous. Added to this he wasn't the easiest of babies, crying every evening from 6pm till late. But I loved him passionately and was very proud of his every achievement. Two and a half years later in January 1974 our second son, Aaron, was born and though he was a very large baby, it was a much faster and much easier delivery, which I was almost able to enjoy. A calmer baby, maybe reflecting my more confident attitude, Aaron was easier to care for and though Adam was a little jealous initially, I worked hard at getting the two little boys to become close to each other.

I loved my boys deeply, and the joy that they bought to my life easily negated the difficulties of bringing up two babies without a mother to hand, and with a husband who considered his duty stopped at conception. However, the cracks were beginning to show. Once again I was visiting my GP on and off telling him of tears and feeling low. I had a sense of hopelessness within me and a deep inexplicable sorrow.

THE FLOOD

In my mind
I picture an ocean

And I know
With a startling clarity
That I have more tears in me than could fill that ocean
A lifetime of tears never cried
But held inside

And I know
There is no future in crying
Crying never helps

But just now I begin to wonder if I can keep it in
Holding onto the hurt for so long
Allowing it to keep hurting
Keep reminding
Every new experience not quite new
But bringing with it memories of an older one
In another time
When I was younger – was I ever young?
My head became old long before my body

There is a dam
The top just below the level of my eyes
Inside my head
The water laps at the edge
And if it burst
The flood of tears
Would never be able to be halted
Not in a lifetime
Not ever

As long as the ocean remains calm I can control it
But like Canute

Though I may try to order it
If the surface is disturbed
Whipped up by swirling currents of memory
The angry, white capped waves
Will tip inexorably over and over
Until
Reaching the utmost edge
They will no longer be held
They will crash
Over the edge
Flooding

And the pretence that is my strong and ordered life
Will be washed away in its path
Destroyed and torn from its roots
In the waters' flood
Scattered all about in a million tiny pieces of flotsam
Leaving a bare and endless landscape where once there was life

Redrawing the map
Of the world that I know
Familiar
Safe
Where all the paths I must take
Are easily negotiated

I struggle for control
Forcing back the threatened flood
Denying its healing rush
Still too afraid
To swim in those muddy waters
To take the chance
To strike out for the other side of my pain
Not yet understanding
That there
And only there
I will find
The peace and serenity that I long for

My GP was an arrogant man, seemingly regarding patients as a necessary evil on his path to a comfortable retirement. His offhand manner did nothing to encourage me to talk about my problems. A gentle enquiring mind may have helped me to start to talk, and possibly to uncover a deeper reason for my unhappiness. Help at that stage could have prevented a great deal of suffering in the years to come. He prescribed Librium, probably assuming that I was suffering from post-natal depression.

I couldn't talk to Philip. He was not a sensitive person, as his childhood had forged him into a tough character, and he did not find it easy to discuss emotional problems. Added to the male preference for the ostrich resolution to all problems this meant that he was unable either to understand or to help me. I think he had experienced many traumatic incidents between his parents in his early childhood, and had shut them out, learning to switch off any outward show of feelings. I had nowhere to run and no-one else to turn to, and it was only through drawing on my inner strength and determination that I held things together. The demands of bringing up two little boys, as well as taking a gradually more active part in our expanding business filled my days and nights, and left little time for reflection. Philip was out most days, two nights a week at training, and playing rugby all day and evening on Saturday. So I was left to order my little world of home and children pretty much as I wished.

Soon after Aaron was born we moved out of the bungalow to a house that we had designed and built on a piece of land at the end of the same cul-de-sac in which we lived. Happy in our new home, the boys growing and starting school, the business expanding, life on the surface appeared good.

My life revolved around the house, the business and caring for my husband and children, so I still relied on Philip for social stimulation. In spring and summer the sunshine and long days lifted my spirits. Childhood memories of sunny days, visits to the seaside, games on the beach, times when I knew that I was safe from any unwanted attention have probably contributed to my positive feeling about the summer. Philip and I spent every weekend we could at the coast water-skiing with friends, and as we now owned a small holiday caravan we were able to travel down on Friday night and stay until Sunday evening. The boys had both been out in the boat from their earliest weeks of life, adapting easily to days playing on the sandbanks, picnics and splashing around in the sea.

Winters were a different matter altogether, and to this day I dread the turn of the year into the long dark months ahead through November, December, January and February. My spirits sink and I become more needy of loving and human contact. Unfortunately this low period for me coincided with the rugby season. Philip's Saturdays were sacrosanct, rugby taking up all day and most of the evening. He insisted that we did not arrange social events for Saturday before 8pm, and even then would often arrive home later, making us late for the dinner or party. I assumed he did it deliberately, and so rows ensued. I became very angry at what I perceived as Philip's selfish attitude to our weekends. His priorities had not changed with the arrival of our children. I tried to explain, to make him understand, that I needed us to have an interest enjoyed together, aside from work and the children. But he refused to make any changes to his lifestyle.

So the cracks in our relationship continued to appear and to deepen. His answer was to stay out more, drink more, and above all maintain his priorities. Even within my busy life I became lonely, resentful and more frustrated with my failure to make our relationship happy. 'Happy' that is, in my perception. I think that Philip was happy enough with the relationship; after all his life had barely changed.

But the blame cannot all lie with Philip's dogged determination to keep his independence. The truth was that I had an emotional hole in me, a need that Philip was incapable of filling. Not because he wouldn't but because he couldn't. The abused little girl in me was desperate to be adored, needing to be actively loved, spoiled and cuddled. She was crying out for the love that she had missed.

And I was changing, maturing, less content with being the follower and accepting others' dominance. In an environment where I was not being abused, I was testing the boundaries, pushing them wider as a child does in normal development, with the result that I was growing and developing too quickly, destroying our relationship with my inexpressible needs, expanding out of control.

Nevertheless he was my husband; I had made a commitment and somehow I just had to make it work. I was determined to succeed, but little did I know that all my attempts were doomed. They had been doomed even before we married. I had fallen in love with him because he was the only person in the world who cared for me. He had supplied me with a lifeline and I had grabbed it. Because of the very lifeline he had thrown I had grown and developed. Now I no longer needed it, and we could neither of us find a replacement: a new springboard for our love.

CHAPTER 14

The deep, unsatisfied longing in me grew. The boys were growing older, spending more time in after school activities, and becoming more independent. Though my relationship with them was close and loving, they were naturally growing away from me in their needs, as children should do. Trying to fill my life, perhaps to leave no time for reflection or consideration of my unhappiness I became an active member of the Parent Governors' Association at the boys' school and I continued to work hard with Philip at developing the business. By 1977 it had changed from transporting caravans and park homes, to the ownership and operation of park home sites themselves. Our respective lives were filled; mine with the business, children and extra curricular school activities, his with the business and rugby. We were a very successful business partnership, but our personal and emotional relationship was failing.

Desperate to fill the emotional hole in my life, I took the step that many women do, and told Philip that I wanted another baby. This time it was my decision. I wanted a baby badly. We tried to conceive but with no immediate success and as the months went by I became distraught, breaking down into floods of tears every month when my period started. I was thirty-two. I visited our doctor, a new one, younger and more understanding, and he advised me that I should stop worrying, I must expect it to take longer this time. Eventually in 1980, our third child was conceived. Due to the difficulties I had experienced with Adam's birth, our private health insurance agreed to cover the cost of an obstetrician, and of the delivery, at the exclusive Princess Margaret Hospital in Windsor. In the event, our daughter was born after one hour of labour at 1.15am on July 11th 1981.

The arrival of a daughter shocked me, overwhelmed me. I had been convinced that I would have a third boy. I even wanted a boy. Names had been chosen, Ben or Oliver, and anyway, I was used to dealing with the rough and tumble of boys.

MY DAUGHTER

Your daughter won't sleep

The nurse, bending over me in the early morning light
Lay the tiny bundle
Wrapped in a pink, cotton blanket
On the bed next to me
Her tuft of fine black hair
And sleepy eyes
Peeking above the wrapping

My arms reached out
Tentatively
Encircled this miracle
Unsure
I gently kissed the wrinkled forehead

My daughter

Fear and apprehension mingled with the joy I was feeling
For this wondrous gift
How could I, so damaged
So ill-prepared for womanhood, for motherhood
Care for, nurture and love
Without condition
This tiny being, who one day
Would herself become a woman
A mother?

My daughter
I have watched you grow
From baby to toddler
From little girl to teenager
And now so soon I see you blossoming
Slowly
But inevitably

Into a young woman

I have watched you
As you strove to cut the bonds that tied you to me
Like an umbilical cord
To forge your own shape, colours and desires

Through all these short years I have loved you
As no other being
Had God searched the heavens
Or pondered a thousand years
He could not have given a gift more precious
A gift to love and treasure
To succour and protect like a young sapling
Whilst it grew

I see you now
Soon to be leaving the cosy protected world with which I have
tried to surround you
The futile wishes to have my chance again
To do it better
To be wiser
Are breaking my heart

I must learn to lock them away
Not to torture myself with the multitude of self-doubts that
they bring
I must focus my thoughts on what I see before me now
And this I hope will give me the conviction
That this beautiful young woman
Because of, or in spite of my efforts
Is equipped with the tools she will need
To conquer the adversities that life will surely bring

But of all my fears and hopes
One stands alone
Central to her burgeoning womanhood
And only time will show

If I have succeeded
In granting her
The sure knowledge
That the gift of motherhood
Is the most precious that she can ever have

At this time of my life, I do not think that I ever thought about my childhood. I now had children of my own, and my greatest conscious efforts were put into giving them all the love and time that I could. It is sometimes said that each successive generation tries to give their children what they felt that they missed out on. But I did not ever think 'I will not abuse my children'. The memories of the abuse that I had suffered at my father's hands were still lying deep within me. This is difficult to explain to someone who has no experience of abuse, because the normal hurts and painful experiences that life brings can more often than not easily be recalled and discussed or shared with close friends. But sexual abuse is something so awful, so terribly damaging that it gets buried deeply, away from all conscious thought. There was no conscious decision to bury the memories; I believe it is an emotional response or mechanism that we use to avoid our having to relive those terrible experiences, to prevent them from ever coming to the surface of our active mind. And even though I was suffering from bouts of depression, and some inexplicable sadness and longing, I still did not make the link between these aspects of my character and my childhood abuse. The memories were entrenched, somewhere in my psyche, buried but not dead, quiet but not stilled, like a cancer, slowly but surely growing, invading and in turn, manipulating and affecting my conscious everyday thought. The abused child lives on in the adult woman; her needs for unconditional love still screaming for satisfaction, her anger surging and boiling like the red hot lava deep within the volcano, waiting to be released, her feelings of an injustice needing validation. For victims of childhood sexual abuse, the old adage: "Out of sight, out of mind", simply does not hold true.

During the early years of marriage I had kept in touch with my parents; the pretence of a normal healthy relationship being precariously sustained. Philip was quite unaware that there was anything untoward in my relationship with my father, and I had not intimated anything unusual. I had a need to establish a family, which included grandparents. My parents' visits were few and far between, the excuse always that my father could not stay away from home. If they ever stayed overnight, they were always up and away first thing in the morning, often before we were even out of bed. Nevertheless, during these short and infrequent visits, I went to extremes to make them feel welcome, cleaning the house from top to bottom and cooking elaborate meals. From time to time, we would take the boys to visit them. I was always excited, returning to my childhood home, proud of my new family, anxious to show them how well my life had turned out, and how happy I was. On one occasion, long before we had decided to have a third child, I had even allowed the boys to stay with my parents for a few days. Proof indeed that I had blanked out the abuse. My overriding memory of these interactions between us was that I still desperately wanted their love and approval.

So it was only natural that I wanted to take their new granddaughter to see them. How proud I was of my new daughter, how beautiful and precious she was. And the boys adored her. Adam, at ten years, had assumed the role of little father. Aaron, a little less sure of how to handle his new sister, catalogued each of her new tricks with pride. My mother had not seen Katie as yet. Ten days after Katie was born, I was taken urgently back into hospital for a D&C, and she had been unable (or unwilling?) to re-arrange her busy schedule to come and help. Philip's sister Kathy, herself the mother of two little girls, and with more than enough problems of her own, travelled all the way up from Plymouth to look after Katie for the night that I was in hospital – much to my relief, as there really was no-one else who I would trust to love and care for my baby girl. I recall that it was the weekend that Princess Diana and Charles were wed, and the day of my return from hospital we cooked a large family meal and watched the proceedings on television.

Perhaps by this time Philip was beginning to wonder why I so needed my parents to be a part of my life; to any outsider it must have been apparent that the giving was all one way.

Nevertheless, on a bright summer Sunday, we packed all three children into the car and drove to Kent to visit my parents and introduce them to their first granddaughter.

NEW BABY

A woman now
Children of her own
Boys
And then, beyond expectation
A girl
A baby girl
What miracle has given her this gift?
Such trust, such innocent need
Total dependence on her
For love, nurture and protection

He rises from his chair in the dark corner
A tall man
Unfolding, leaning forward
Menacing?
Threatening?
Arms outstretched
To encompass the child

A smile of anticipation
He takes the child from her

Something wrong
Badly wrong

As she hands the child over
The joy disappears
Replaced by an icy panic
She wants to snatch back the precious new life
A part of her body
Innocent, uncontaminated
As yet

But he turns and holds the child to his breast
His back turned to her

Unable to control the hot rushing storm
Surging up from deep inside her
She turns
Runs out of the room
Upstairs
To the bathroom
Familiar
Where another child, long ago
Was touched and damaged

Head over the white porcelain bowl
Her insides revolting
Turning inside out
Retching, vomiting
Surging, unstoppable
The pressure of years of denial
Of coping, suppressing
Pouring forth in one violent, foul stream

The lid is lifted
This well will not be capped
Until the anger is resolved
The hurt offered balm
And the grief for so much that was lost
Assuaged

The traumatic experience I had when I took Katie to Kent was the catalyst that was needed, the key to the locked memories. Poured into the mix of the failing relationship with my husband, the reaction began, the clock was set and ticking inexorably down to zero hour. From that day I knew that I could not ever let Katie be left alone with my father and thus my mother's inevitable questions as to why we would not allow her to come and stay as the boys had done became more and more difficult to answer. Philip accepted my vague answers that it was not convenient, that it did not fit with our family plans.

Through the boys' school we had made friends, some of whom we met socially as a couple, and others, just girl friends whom I would meet occasionally for coffee or lunch. I formed long term relationships with only one or two. It is these same friends – two in particular – Anne and Mary, who have stood by me through the difficult years that were to follow the opening of the Pandora's Box that held the tragic secrets of my past. I count myself lucky to have them, two people whom I can count on, no matter what.

Anne had two boys of her own, one the same age as Aaron and another slightly younger. We had met and chatted whilst waiting outside the school doors to collect our boys and something had clicked between us. We lunched occasionally, and our friendship grew, steadily and slowly, never all embracing, or exclusive to others because Anne always had many friends and acquaintances. Not a great social animal myself, I was satisfied with one or two close friends, though I did not expect anyone to cleave themselves to me alone.

Mary came into my life a little later, when Katie started school. She also had a Katie, her only child, and we shared the school run, and soon became friends. We were and still are two quite different women, but, opposites attract, and we have to this day a very firm friendship.

And what of my grandparents, those darling people who had been such a steady, loving influence during my childhood and teenage years? My grandmother had taken to Philip, finding him 'solid' and 'decent'. When visiting Kent, I had always tried to include some time at their house. The boys too came to love that house, full of evocative smells and sights, and her home-made cakes. Once or maybe twice a year we invited them up to stay a few days with us. I loved having them, and looked forward immensely to their visits. Taking them out to experience new things was one of my great joys – tea at Harrods, trips to the theatre, shopping in Kingston, we crammed as much into their few days as we could. I think I was subconsciously repaying them for all they had done for me. More important though, they were family without strings, without hidden unpleasant relationships, and their love for me, and my new family was priceless.

All of these important people have formed a chain of support throughout my life. So at almost every stage there has been some loving input, someone who cared enough to provide shelter from the storms when they hit. They have been my salvation. I cannot over emphasise the value of their contribution to my becoming the woman that I am. But there is one person who contributed more than any other; one being, one child, one woman; the one who triggered the chain reaction and then had to deal with the consequences.

CHAPTER 15

In June 1982 when Katie was a year old we moved again, this time to a beautiful old house in Sunningdale, set in two acres of gardens. The house was very large, the original small cottage having been extended, reputedly with a Lutyens design, earlier in the century. There were more than enough bedrooms for five of us to spread out, with a beautifully proportioned sitting room and dining room, and gardens that the children could lose themselves in. It was the perfect home for raising our young family and entertaining friends, and to all outward appearance we were the ideal family.

But the patch that Katie had been meant to provide over the tear in our marital relationship was temporary and frail. Far more was needed. A patch will only hold if the edges of the tear to which it is fixed are strong. Our tear was not a single clean cut from the outside. It was a rupture from within, growing, splitting and fraying at the edges; the damage inbuilt before the first union of the fabric of our marriage.

An abused child has had her boundaries violated. She becomes a disproportionate force within the adult mind, fearing that those boundaries will be violated again and again. To counteract this fear the adult develops a need to control, to ensure that the boundaries by which she sets her standards are not violated. This need becomes a dominant force and permeates every aspect of the adult life. I can recognise this aspect of my character and realise the strong part it played in my everyday actions and decisions.

THE WOMAN CHILD

Innocence
Obliterated
Stolen and discarded

By whose right?

Never to be recaptured
Rediscovered
Never possible now to know the freshness of new joys
Of learning by self experiment

Innocence
Destroyed forever
For the selfish gratification of perverted desire
By the power of one being over another
Power given in trust
And used in abuse of that trust

Childhood denied
By those who, most of all, should have given it willingly
With love and care
To nurture the seed
Until it grew to womanhood

The pain of that loss never diminishing
With the passage of time
But remaining a lifelong curse
The little girl ever present in the woman
Begging for recognition
A chance to cleanse her of the filth and guilt
Of a childhood that never was
Begging for the love that was never given

Why?
The question will never be answered
Her guilt feeding on their denial

Those precious years wasted
Force-fed with all the perversions and desires of a sick adult
mind
Used up ahead of time
The child that should have been
Never was
Always knowing that she was different from the others
Standing apart
Unable to find the common thread
With which to weave the natural fabric of childhood friendships

The little girl lives on in the woman
Tearing her in two
Haunting her
An ever-present ghost, shadowing the adult life
Every decision
Every judgement
Made by the woman?
Yet influenced by the child?

My confidence had grown through my success in running my side of the business, and with organising functions for the children's schools. In all of these activities I was able to maintain a great deal of control. So it was only a matter of time before I began to question Philip's control over our joint marital decisions.

Philip avoided confrontation, and kept a tight rein on his emotions. He had learned that he needed to be in control to deal with life, and he applied this logic to our relationship. Our marriage therefore became a tug of war, each of us trying to prevent the other from pulling them over a midway line where the boundaries were drawn. Each was convinced that their position was the correct one – the only one from which they could function and maintain their self-respect.

I attempted to explain my unhappiness to Philip on several occasions I can recall specifically. I chose the timing carefully, not wishing to add my words to an already developing argument that we may have been having. Each time his reaction was simply to put an arm around me and offer platitudes to the effect that I would feel better in the morning, or he would offer to take me out for dinner, as though he could put a sticking plaster over my hurt and it would then heal itself, undercover, with no further need of salve from him. My hurts and needs within a relationship were being dismissed all over again, not considered to be valid or important. He had no idea that he was pouring fuel onto a smouldering fire.

The boys continued to flourish, doing all the normal healthy things that boys should do. There was only one black cloud in the sky of my sons' lives as far as I was concerned. It was expected that at age eleven boys would become full time boarders at their prep school. I was heartbroken when the time came for Adam to go into this new regime, and I cried every night for months. Each Sunday evening when I stood at the end of the drive, waving at the car as it slowly disappeared into the distance, taking him back to school, my heart broke. I had to cope once more with this heartbreak when Aaron joined him two years later.

My relationship with the boys had been easy, comfortable and fun. I had no pre-determined expectations of them, so they could not let me down. With Katie the relationship was different. As she grew from a baby to a toddler and then a little girl, a desire in me to give her all that I had not received, developed and intensified. What I had not received, of course, was natural, healthy parental love. The manifestation of these needs in me encompassed everything that I could provide her with – pretty dresses and shoes (remember the black lace ups?), beautiful long hair (remember the short pudding bowl?), piano lessons, dancing lessons, ice skating lessons, pet rabbits and extravagant parties for her school friends, each birthday. But the love she needed. Was it there, freely available? Only she can answer that. I was demanding, expecting her to do well at school – failure was not an option. She particularly struggled with math, the subject that I found easy, and I was unable to explain the intricacies of these rows of figures in a way that she could grasp. My frustration showed: I often became angry and cruelly rapped her knuckles with her rule one evening when she failed to understand the complexities of long division. I wanted so much for her – why could she not see this? The guilt I felt afterwards is indescribable – I was abusing my own child – all because she could not live up to my expectations for her. Were they for her, or for me though? Was I trying to prove that I could raise a well-rounded and successful woman, as opposed to the one that my parents had reared?

As ever, Philip was calm and unperturbed. Not good at maths himself he could empathise with his daughter and tried to placate us both. He did not berate me but tried to make me see that maybe she would just not be a mathematician. He adored his little girl, his little princess, and could no more smack her or make her cry, than fly to the moon. Whatever she did he would be happy for her. I had no concerns about their relationship. It was perfectly normal: she had a loving devoted father and he an adoring daughter. Bath-times for her with her daddy were a joy, full of fun and laughter – I remember him telling me that she had bounced on the bed in front of him, stark naked, teasing him, squealing with laughter, when he was trying to catch her to dry her and dress her in her pyjamas. He would look at me quizzically when I asked him – no told him – be careful when you wash her, you know – her bottom, don't you do it, let her wash it herself. Signs indeed that the memory deep within me was stirring, gradually awakening and unfolding in preparation for rebirth and destruction of its host. But though I had no fears of hidden aspects in their relationship, I began to experience uncomfortable feelings of envy. Envy that she had something I had never had, nor could ever have. Something that I still desperately wanted, needed, the missing something that had created the void in me that could never be filled. I would never be anybody's little princess.

Katie was around six or seven when I started to suffer from terrible skin irritation. The first bout started late one November, and lasted through till spring. It eased during the summer but returned again next winter, and was more severe the second time around. Mainly occurring in the evenings, it would continue most of the night. The skin on my lower legs and feet suffered the most. Terrible itching, relentless, like an army of ants crawling around under my skin, but with no outward physical signs. I would remove my tights, place my feet in a bowl of cold water, and scratch and scratch, feeling as though I needed to tear away several layers of my skin to make it stop, even though common sense was telling me that the more I scratched, the more it would irritate. Concerned and helplessly watching me claw myself until my legs and feet were bleeding, Philip tried to stop me from scratching, to no avail. Visits to the GP proved fruitless as I had nothing to show them; nothing that is except the deep scratch-marks, scabs and scars on my legs. Regularly, in the middle of the night I would leave our bed and stand under an ice cold shower to try to gain relief. One doctor suggested I might have an allergy to soap powder. I changed the brand to a baby sensitive one. No difference. Another suggested it might be a food allergy, as they did not necessarily manifest themselves as stomach complaints. This time I visited a food allergy specialist who tested me and gave me lists of food to cut out. By late January I was existing on potato and pineapple alone. Never particularly heavy, my weight started to drop and I became even slimmer, raising compliments more than questions.

Alongside the development of my physical discomfort, was a growing emotional problem coinciding in time and depth. I began to have disturbing flashes of my father's face when Philip made love to me. Gradually I began to reject his touch, finding it easier to turn my back on him than to explain what I was feeling. And in any case my itching was such that any added heat increased its intensity and my discomfort. Philip did not complain, he could see that I was suffering, and probably decided that it would eventually improve. He did not look for any deeper meaning to my problems. As long as I could function pretty much as normal, there could not be anything seriously wrong – could there?

I knew that I was unwell, really unwell. But I could not fathom why or what. I had still made no connection between these current problems and my childhood abuse, or my feelings regarding Katie's place in my husband's life. Nevertheless, the symptoms of my internal strife were manifesting themselves in a physical manner and I felt that the strings that held my life together were steadily becoming unravelled. More and more I was operating as an automaton, able to fulfil my role as wife, mother, housewife and business partner with an almost robotic mechanism, functioning perfectly well but without any feelings. I felt neither joy, nor any desire to laugh. The sense of fun in anything I did was becoming a memory. And gradually, unnoticed, the confidence that I had been able to gain over the past years began to dissolve.

The underlying reason of food sensitivity was the easiest to believe and one that I could hopefully alleviate, given the right advice. Eventually the GP put me in touch with a specialist in London. I went to see him and after a series of questions, and only one visit, he explained gently to me that he thought that my illness was psychosomatic. By this time my weight was down to 7st 10lb. (I am 5ft 6ins tall and look best around 9st 7lb.)

I was often tired and generally irritable and as the boys were now away at boarding school, Katie was left alone to bear the brunt. She came home from school one day and asked me if I had cancer, because one of her friends had overheard her mother discussing me with another mother. They had assumed that my drastic weight loss was due to cancer. These comments, the guilt over my treatment of Katie, my physical illness, the gradual breakdown of my relationship with Philip and the inexplicable feelings of envy all combined and built up steam like a pressure cooker. The lid finally blew early in 1990.

Philip had gone away to the rugby final at Cardiff, leaving me alone in the house with Katie. I had begged him not to go. I think I knew that the edge of the precipice was racing up towards me. Late on Saturday morning, shaking, feeling that my legs would buckle beneath me and with a sense that I just wanted to shut down, I called Anne, and told her, "I cannot cope, please come, I cannot manage on my own here with Katie." What she thought I do not know, because I don't recall that we had ever discussed my problems in any depth. She came immediately, took one look at me and called the doctor. By the time he arrived I was sitting in a chair, rocking backwards and forwards, pretty much incoherent, with Anne trying to contact Philip, and to comfort Kate.

The volcano had erupted; the long years of rumbling away beneath the surface, of gently pushing at the crust that had taken years to form had come to an end. An end that would not bring healing; not for a long time. An end that would in itself, be the beginning of a long and difficult journey. The eruption must be allowed to continue, relentlessly, spewing out the muck, the destructive force that had for years been burning away inside.

Chapter 16

I recall very little of that Saturday afternoon. I know that Philip was finally located, and told by Anne, that no, it couldn't wait until the next morning, he must come home immediately.

I can see me, sitting in a chair in the corner of the playroom, softly crying and rocking backward and forward, my hands gripping the seat. The doctor is kneeling on his haunches in front of me, a concerned look on his face, his soft voice calming me. How lucky for me that he was not a 'pull yourself together' man! What did I tell him? Were there revealing fragments of information teased out by his gentle probing? Did he give me a sedative? I know that I was totally incapable of functioning at any normal level. Perhaps my mind had simply switched off, and gone into shutdown as a means of survival, no longer able to deal with the demands being placed upon it by my seething emotions.

That weekend, our friends Dawn and Mick, who were now living and working in the West Midlands, were visiting relatives in the Sunningdale area. Dawn has told me that for some reason, a last minute decision, they called in on us on the Sunday morning. She vividly recalls arriving at the back entrance to the house, and seeing me sitting on the back staircase; pale gaunt face, eyes flickering around in fear, my hands sticking out from a large baggy jumper, my fingers nervously picking at the sleeve ends. She could not believe what she was seeing, and having asked Philip what on earth had happened, was told that it was nothing to worry about and that I would be alright within a few days. Sadly, this reply typified Philip's total lack of comprehension of my problems and how deep rooted they were, let alone how dramatically they might affect our relationship. Perhaps because he did not want to face up to the enormity of what was happening to his hitherto competent and capable wife. Or, more likely, because he was just not capable of understanding the intensity of this manifestation of my emotional damage. I know it wasn't that he did not care that I was unwell, just that he did not appreciate the seriousness of the problem.

The doctor, however, was concerned enough to arrange for Philip and me to receive some professional help in the form of counselling. I must have said something that afternoon that made him realise that this was more than just a case of an over-tired mother. When we made the first visit together, we saw two people: John and Daphne. I think that the idea of having a man and a woman was that neither of us would feel unsupported or outnumbered. Though our marriage was discussed and both of us were able to express our views, I am sure it became obvious to them that I needed more help. Philip, never happy with discussing emotional problems, was probably quite relieved with the proposal that I should continue alone with therapy.

They suggested that I should meet with John, for further discussion. I refused; I could not talk to a man, as a man was the source of my problem. At that particular time, to my mind 'a man' equated to Philip. I had no comprehension of the real cause of my condition. I needed a woman to talk to, someone who would empathise with me, understand my feelings and give me the answers I needed. How could a man possibly do that? My request was refused, gently, but firmly. It was explained that the very fact that it was a man that had caused my hurt meant that I should be able to let my feelings of anger out towards a man for them to be validated. Had I said anything about my father at that point? I do not know. But couched in their advice to me was their professional knowledge of a strong probability that the hurt went much further back than my marriage. And so I agreed to meet with John on a weekly basis, with no real appreciation of what it would entail in the way of emotional effort and input, and what the likely outcome would be. Neither did I have any idea whatsoever of the length of the journey that I was embarking on. Despite my initial resistance to him, John proved to be one of the most important people in the following six years of my life. Years later he told me that he had a pretty good idea quite early on that somewhere along the journey my marriage to Philip would be a casualty.

In the event, our marriage struggled on for another three years.

My abuse was embedded deep within me, a dark shameful secret, the details too awful to be shared with anyone. But as my meetings with John progressed, I began to trust him; his gentle coaxing gradually enabling me to talk, to finally share the dreadful burden of shame and guilt that I had been carrying for so many years. But still I filtered the information, testing his reactions. I told him first of the bath times, expecting revulsion and disgust to be reflected back on me. But he explained gently that the shame was not mine, that the guilt was not mine to bear. Slowly but surely, in this safe environment I was able to tell him more details of the abuse, though still hanging onto what I considered the worst until much later, sometimes finding it too embarrassing to use the words needed to express what had happened. However, I was able to release my anger with no fear of retribution, to be able to say exactly how I felt with no fear of judgement, and most importantly to have my anger validated. And I cried, slowly and controlled at first, until I knew it was safe, but in time a torrent of tears poured out, the pressure lessening with the release of the anguish of painful memories.

Philip took the view that this was just treatment for a condition, in the same way that an antibiotic will treat and cure a sore throat. Life would carry on as normal, with the patient maybe needing a few days off to recuperate. The emotional effort required for each session was draining, both mentally and physically and I always felt exceptionally tired for the following day or two. But our life continued along the same lines as before.

During this time, Adam left school, spent two years at college, then started to work with us, as well as spending some time travelling in the USA. Aaron completed his A-levels, and spent nine months travelling in Australia and then completed a sound engineering course before going to university to read media studies.

And what of my little girl, Kate, the baby who had been the catalyst that had set this train of events in motion? During this difficult period of home life, she managed somehow to continue working hard at school, learning to play the piano and the violin, and to start singing with the church choir.

All three of my children had been taught to play the piano by Eileen Stearn, a wonderful Christian lady who was loved by all her pupils. I had previously told her of my unfulfilled, and hitherto unvoiced, yearning as a child to learn to play the piano. Her reply was quite simple "It's never too late!" So I visited her weekly for piano lessons, and I enjoyed them immensely. After Katie was born my lessons had gradually stopped, because I was finding it difficult to fit in practice times with the demands of our growing business and family, but by then my relationship with Eileen had developed into friendship.

Through the years Eileen has become one of the stalwarts of my life, always there to listen, and talk through anything that is bothering me. She carries about her person an aura of peace and calm, and her home is a haven from the cares of the world. I have grown to love her, and in my heart she has become the mother that I might have had. It was clear that she had a strong faith, which prompted me to question her about God and she answered with the conviction that only a committed and practising Christian can. Her responses encouraged the gradual rebirth in me of a belief. A belief which had been shattered when my father told me, when I was still very young, that there was no such thing as God. He told me that as a small boy he had once asked God to strike him dead. Because He hadn't, my father concluded that God did not exist.

It was early in 1992 that I experienced again the sad loss of someone whom I loved dearly. During the eighties my darling grandmother had become progressively debilitated by dementia. I lived a considerable distance from my grandparents, and did not see them often, but was in touch through my brother Robert. Her condition was dramatically brought home to me when we did eventually visit her. She was forgetful of where she had put things, even why she had gone into the kitchen. Worst of all for me, the house was dirty, an indication that something was radically wrong. My grandfather, who since the birth of my children had been nicknamed 'Gramps', was no longer able to cope with her tantrums, nor her refusal to get dressed each morning. Social services had advised my mother that she needed to go into a home. Gramps was desolate; they had been together for more than sixty years. It was agreed that we should find a place where they could both go, and though he was reluctant to give up his home, Gramps accepted that it would be the only way that they could remain together.

I left it to my mother to find a suitable home, and was delighted when very quickly she called to say that she had located exactly the right place. Gramps would stay there for a few days' trial, whilst my grandmother went into hospital for some tests. I drove down to Kent to visit him in his new home and it was quite awful. There was a pervading smell of boiled cabbage, and the day room was a mean, small room at the rear of the building, having only one high window, so no outlook. He stood in his bedroom, and looked at me, tears glistening in his rheumy eyes.

"Please don't make me stay here."

Choking back tears, I left him. But later, I asked my mother why on earth she had chosen that place. Her answer was that it was convenient for them to visit. Convenient for my father to drop in on the way to the pub more like! She finally admitted that there was a slightly better one, but it was a further ten miles away; too far to drive. I took Gramps to see it, and the difference was immeasurable. It had recently been fully refurbished, and every communal room had views across the estuary. Mr Yong, the Chinese proprietor, assured me that Gran and Gramps could have adjacent bedrooms, and that he would keep them both until the end. His policy was not to push them into nursing homes, even if they became difficult to manage.

Gramps liked this home, and I was certainly much happier for my darling grandparents to stay here, so the arrangements were made, and they moved in. Mr Yong was true to his word, caring for them both very well.

Gran's funeral was simple. As she was eighty-eight there were very few mourners. We sang 'All things bright and beautiful', a hymn which I associate with her to this day, and I remembered her singing it when we were children. It was awful, knowing that she was no longer in this world, knowing that never again would I feel her cuddling me, or breathe in her evocative grandma smell. Gramps survived her by two years and died almost to the day in March 1994. The last link to the only loving and caring environment in my childhood had been severed.

In September 1992 Kate moved to a girls' boarding school, which meant that Philip and I were left together most of the weekday evenings. It made little difference; we did not take advantage of this newfound freedom. By this time he had stopped playing rugby, finding his weekly injuries did not heal in time for the following weekend game. In its place he had taken up golf. In an effort to find something that we could enjoy together I started to learn to play also, but my heart was not in it. However, there was no opportunity to establish a new aspect of our relationship as Philip insisted that I took lessons and practised on my own, at the local nine-hole course. The result was more frustration, and I am sure Kate can regale her friends with tales of my anger spilling out onto the golf course. My instructor once summed it up: "You are meant to hit the ball smoothly and move it out into an arc, Jacki, not beat the shit out of it!"

Our business relationship continued to be successful. Having always been a sun lover, I managed to persuade Philip to buy a holiday apartment in Spain. I think the scales were tipped by the fact that the apartment overlooked a brand new golf course! We had discovered Puerto de la Duquesa four years previously when visiting some old friends who had settled there, and fallen in love with the small Spanish fishing port, which had been tastefully extended to include a marina, low rise apartment blocks, restaurants and bars. Our apartment had stunning views, down to Gibraltar on a clear day, and overlooked the ninth hole on the golf course. Ownership of an apartment automatically included membership of the golf club. It was a beautiful apartment, and once again we were able to put our energies into a new project, thus being able to ignore the ever-widening fault lines in our relationship. But the anticipation of happier times spent together in our wonderful, new second home was a false dawn.

CHAPTER 17

Katie's departure to boarding school was the final straw. My hysterectomy in 1989 meant no more babies, no new love to fill my empty heart. By mid 1993 my life had become so empty and meaningless that I found it hard even to get out of bed in the mornings. And my visits to John were becoming less frequent. We had reached a plateau. I think John knew there were more mountains for me to climb, but I felt that I had released my anger, told as much about the abuse that I could remember and that was about as far as it could go. When we discussed a halt in the programme he told me that he believed that there was much more that lay buried, but that maybe he was not the right person to bring it out. In a strange way I had come to love him, not in an inappropriate way, but as the first man in my life who did not tell me what I should or should not do or feel about any given situation. Whilst we both acknowledged that we had reached a staging post, a place to stop and take stock – almost to wait and see what would happen next – I think he understood that I was still in a mess, and that my 'healing journey' was barely begun.

It was at one of our last meetings that I told him that I thought that I might leave Philip. I had tested him, hoping for a decisive answer that would guide me. And though not categorically a yes or no, he gave me the answer I needed.

"If you truly believe that you would be happier on your own in a little attic flat, than you are now with Philip and all that you have materially, then yes you could go."

And my vague thoughts began to form into a resolution that I actually could leave, and survive.

It is of little consolation to me that it was Philip's hand holding the hammer that drove the final nail into the coffin of our marriage. But I can, without doubt, pinpoint the day, the hour, almost the minute that I knew my decision had been made.

During the summer of 1993, within the limitations of the school holidays, we had taken every opportunity to use our lovely new apartment in Spain. The apartment complex had been marketed extensively in the UK and consequently many of the customers frequenting the bars, and even running some, were Brits.

One of our favourite bars was owned and run by an English couple and their daughter, Jan, who was a giant of a woman in every sense of the word; an extremely vivacious and attractive redhead with a personality that matched. Jan's bar was popular with the golfing fraternity and the walls were covered with photographs of Jan with famous players. There were small groups of tables inside and out and a row of stools at the bar, which was almost always full; after golf, after work, after dinner, late evening and sometimes into the early hours of the morning. Over and above the mix of voices Jan's deep husky tones could always be heard. She was the centre of action, overseeing everything, aware of who had paid and who had not, washing glasses, pouring drinks, and often holding two conversations or more at the same time. I once saw her lean over the bar and grab a man by the collar, with two hands, almost lifting him off his feet, demanding loudly that he pay up, then leave. She clearly thought that he had already had more than enough to drink, and wanted him out. I liked Jan; found her friendly and easy to chat to, often sitting at the bar chatting with her whilst Philip discussed the day's golf with his friends.

Another man entered my life that summer; a relationship that would create one of the most tempestuous years of my life, and prove to be the mechanism that finally triggered the breakdown. Was there a guiding hand, slowly but irrevocably reaching into my life and propelling it headlong onto the road along which I had to travel in order to finally become free of the legacy of my childhood? The force that drew me towards him was powerful, almost tangible.

Philip and I had arranged to meet at Jan's bar with two friends for a pre-dinner drink. Bending slightly as I walked down the stairs I sensed rather than saw someone looking at me.

ENCOUNTER

Raw Sex
Animal Scent
Nostrils quivering
Where?

Eyes lifted, flicker over the crowd
Meeting
There!

One deep, seemingly never ending encounter
Penetrating
Warm liquid eyes
Melting
Commanding attention
I am here
I want you

Blinding, in that second
Desire so strong
Primal urges long buried
Rise torrentially
Like a flash flood
Destroying all in its path

Swept along in the rushing waters
Over the edge
Crashing, tumbling downward
Twisting and turning
At the mercy of these raging senses

No denying this overwhelming passion
No way back
The exit locked
Key thrown away

Life as you know it
Ended

A brief instant, but one that would prove cataclysmic. Our eyes met, pulled away, and then I was back with my husband and friends. I thought no more of him immediately, but later, I felt curiosity. Who was he?

Kate and I would pass our days by the pool, me reading, whilst she swam and played with the other children. Some days we would walk down to the port for an ice cream, or a hot chocolate at our favourite bar on the front line of the port and enjoy a lazy hour watching the boats and people, busy in the marina. One day, the man I had seen in the bar stopped at our café, and asked if he might join us. Since Kate was with me I saw no harm in having a coffee with a stranger. He introduced himself; he was Fritz, Dutch, a retired psychologist, living on a large schooner in the marina. His wife had died of cancer two years before. He was attractive, there was no doubt that I found him so, but in strange way I also felt that he was dangerous, and perhaps that strengthened the attraction. There was a darkness about him that was not just due to his swarthy good looks. We started to meet often, but always with Kate there between us, unwittingly acting as the safety net, the barrier that held my rushing emotions in place.

I told Philip about him, there was no reason not to, but I suspect that in telling Philip I was trying to convince myself that the friendship was innocent. My daughter was with me, and my husband knew of him. He was just an acquaintance. Fritz was never other than impeccably polite and correct, never touching me, but there was a frisson between us; a powerful force of which we were both aware. It was exciting and certainly a diversion from my unhappiness. However, I must have mentioned his name once too often, for one day, unexpectedly, when I had told Philip that Fritz had invited Kate and me to look over his yacht, he announced that he would not be playing golf but would be coming with us. And he did, listening to every word that was said, looking with feigned interest at every part of the engine, sailing equipment and storage facilities as Fritz proudly showed us around, explaining the intricacies of the beautiful yacht that he had built.

One Saturday, at the end of another week when Philip had played golf every day, I was looking forward to going out to dinner, and had taken extra care to look good. He arrived home a little late, a little drunk and told me that he did not want to go out. I was furious, so without stopping to think where I would go, and what I would do on my own, I picked up my handbag and went out alone for the first time since we had married.

I headed for Jan's bar, hoping that she would be there. I was in luck, and as I walked through the door she called out "Hi Jacki". We chatted inconsequentially, and then she asked where Philip was. My reply was short and sharp, leaving her in no doubt that I was out on my own, but looking for company. She had not eaten and asked if I fancied joining her for a pizza in the nearby Italian restaurant during her break. Later, over dinner, I told her something of my circumstances. As a woman who had been very unlucky in love, I think that she understood how I felt, and sensed my loneliness. She encouraged me to be more independent, told me that I could make it on my own, that I was attractive and would easily find friendship and company. Just one hour with her, and only a few words but it reaffirmed the notion that I could survive on my own.

When Jan and I returned to the bar, Fritz was there. He was obviously surprised to find me without my husband. We had a drink together, and without the restraint of Kate's presence, the talk developed into deeper subjects. As a psychologist he was a good listener, and of course he knew how to manipulate the conversation. I soon found myself pouring my heart out to him, unwittingly giving him all the ammunition he would find useful in the future.

That night the balance of my relationship with Philip tipped in my favour. My conviction that I could survive without him strengthened, and I held a tantalising vision of a future free from the suffocating confines of our marriage. There is no doubt that Philip sensed something had changed;

133

he did not once leave me to go out on my own again throughout the holiday.

Two months later I was back in Spain, a pre-arranged holiday with three of my girlfriends. We had a great week and I thoroughly enjoyed showing them the port, the bars and restaurants. But at some point I decided that I would not return with them. I wanted time by myself, to think, to experiment more with being on my own, choosing for myself the times, the places and people I would see. I called Philip and told him that I had changed my flight and was staying for another five days. When I did return it was to tell him that I was leaving him.

During the five days that I stayed on after the girls left, I met Fritz most evenings for a drink. I saw him as a friend, a confidant, somebody who really understood what was troubling me. I guess by the time I returned home there was very little that Fritz did not know about me. He knew that I was thinking of ending my marriage, and had told me that I could call him, if I was feeling low. However, I can still recall the shocked silence that was his response when I did call four weeks later to tell him that I had found an apartment to live in, and my marriage was over. Had he put me down as a woman who would complain and threaten but not follow through? I know he was stunned at how quickly things had moved, and he asked earnestly,

"Are you sure, are you really sure?"

I was, and I knew that whilst he had neither suggested nor persuaded me to make the final decision, he was the last piece in the puzzle. The final figure, adding to the equation, making it balance, making the jumping out as equal as the staying in. I could not be any unhappier out than in.

The few weeks that I remained in the family home with Philip were hell, for both of us. We both cried every night, and would arrive at the office red eyed and weary, lethargic and uninterested in the business that had been the cement of our relationship. It was not difficult for me to tell close girlfriends. I told Anne first and her lack of surprise further supported my decision. Friends who were part of our joint social circle were shocked. Outwardly, I think we were the ideal couple, and the split rocked the foundations of the social group that we moved in. Naturally people took sides, and I quickly found where loyalties lay.

The hardest thing I had to do was to tell Kate. Philip refused to have anything to do with it. His attitude was, "You are the one causing this, you deal with it". I waited until October half term. Taking Kate into the family room, sitting on the sofa with her while Philip stood nervously to one side, looking out of the window as if seeing something there that caught and occupied his attention, I struggled to find the words, to tell her that there was no blame, nobody had been bad, or hurtful, Mummy and Daddy just did not feel the same about each other any more. I was crying before I finished, and to this day I cannot recall her expression that moment. I knew that I had done something that I had never thought I would – hurt one of my children. Her response was to tell us that she wanted to talk to her friend, Nicole, and she left the room to go and telephone her. I felt that, in less than a few moments, I had destroyed the lifetime of trust that my daughter had in her parents. She did not throw herself into either of the waiting pairs of arms that so badly wanted to comfort her, hold her and make her feel better, unwittingly refusing to give them the reassurance that physical contact would bring. She left the room, and we looked at each other helplessly, finding no solace in our own empty hearts.

PART 3: FRITZ

CHAPTER 18

Mick, Philip and myself; compatriots, brothers in arms since 1968, slowly carried the few belongings that I was taking, up the stairs to the small two-bedroom apartment, part of an old house in Sunninghill. Quite a comedown from the luxurious eight-bedroom house that I had just left; as my friend Maureen was at pains to remind me the first time she visited me in my new abode. I knew her marriage was rocky, and she had considered leaving her husband, but she cast her eyes around my tiny flat and commented, "But I'm not this desperate". Small, no garden, no luxuries, but it would be all mine. Rented, but still mine, to come and go as I pleased, to furnish as I pleased, to cook what I wanted, when I wanted.

"Bye Mick, bye Philip." The van reversed out of the driveway, and I gave them a brief goodbye wave. I would of course be seeing Philip again, in the office where we had worked so hard together building up our successful business. But that would be all. At the end of the working day, I would return to my new home and he to the family home. And this only until some financial arrangement could be sorted out, and a replacement for me in the business could be found and trained, and then that would be it – the end of our twenty-five years together.

I watched as Philip and Mick drove away in the small white van that had brought my possessions, and me to my new home. Here I was, having left home for the second time in my life, standing in my own apartment, surrounded by boxes, suitcases and some of the smaller pieces of furniture from our marital home. How did I feel? Frightened? Excited? Probably both of these mixed pretty much in equal proportions. I had what I wanted but I was frightened by the responsibility. Not emotionally or financially, but practically – fearful of the silly, small everyday things like locking up, managing the heating system, being alone in the flat at night; fearful of parking my car in the garage around the rear of the building and walking the fifty yards back to the main door along the unlit pathway. I now understand that I had no real appreciation of the enormity of the step that I had taken in ending a twenty-five year relationship wherein there had been security and safety, with the underlying knowledge that there was someone to share the problems. The effects of my decision manifested themselves every day in problems that I had not previously had to deal with alone. They were challenging but I learned to overcome them, and with each small success, I grew in confidence and the fear abated.

While the fear was in the practicalities of life, the excitement was in the taste of a new experience, of release, of freedom, of not having to account to anyone for my movements, and desires. Emotionally I had always been alone, so there was nothing new to fear there. I had been right though; I was not less happy out of the marriage than in, I was actually happier.

By this time the boys had left home and were relatively independent, and so I felt far less guilt towards them than I did towards Kate. Adam was angry with me and I had to accept his refusal even to try to understand how I could leave his father, who was a star to him, a shining example that he looked up to. Aaron was more pragmatic and supportive. He took the view that I had given twenty-five years of my life to the family, and that if I needed to move on, then I should do so.

With Kate it was different. Being so much younger than the boys she had almost been an only child, and did not have a close enough bond with her brothers to be able to share with them her feelings about this new situation. Philip and I were her world, and we had split it in two. Loving her so much and trying desperately to seek a way forward that would hurt her the least, we agreed that she should have the choice of how to share her home-life between us. On reflection, I realise that perhaps this was not fair, thrusting such a difficult decision upon her. Trying to be meticulously fair she divided her weekends and half terms at home evenly between us. She became a little 'bag lady', packing and unpacking her collection of loved and precious belongings – teddies, pictures, notebooks, all the treasures that every twelve-year-old clings to – every other weekend or four weeks according to where she would be staying. We had no appreciation of the cruelty of this, considering only our needs, each wanting to be with our child, to prove that our separation was working well, really, wasn't it? Ask Kate now and I am sure that she will tell a different story entirely. Each of the three of us saw only one face of the world that we carved. Each face was a necessary part of the whole, but existing in a separate plane.

As Christmas was so near I offered – and Philip accepted – that I should return to the family home for Christmas Day so that we could try to enjoy a family Christmas. It was a struggle for all of us, but we made the most of it.

I continued to work each day, partly because I knew that I needed to earn money, but mainly because I knew that I was a key part of the administration of the business and to have walked out would have caused a major problem. Later, when I took solicitors' advice, it was that I should stay working to ensure that my financial situation would not be prejudiced by any claim that I had deserted the business and reneged on my responsibilities within it. I was determined that the financial separation should be as amicable as possible. We had known of another separation which had ended in a bitter and drawn out dispute over money and property, and I felt strongly that the children should not have to go through the added hurt and indignity of watching their parents fight over money in court.

By mid January 1994, I had been living alone for over two months, and the strain of seeing each other at work every day was beginning to tell on both of us. This daily struggle, in addition to my dislike of winter, made it an easy decision for me to spend a couple of weeks in the apartment in Spain. We had already made some preliminary decisions as to how to divide our estate, and as Philip refused to leave or sell the family home, it had been tacitly agreed that I should, for the meantime at least, have the use of the apartment. I flew out, not quite sure what I was going to do with my time, but the anticipation of a couple of weeks in the sun was enough.

Needing somewhere familiar and safe on my first evening, I decided to visit Jan's bar. It was still quite early, and only one or two people sat in the bar, one of whom was Fritz. He was sitting in his usual corner, on a stool, up at the bar, and when I walked in alone he looked at me, an invitation with his eyes to join him, signalling the stool next to him. It was as though he had been sitting there, in that same place, every night since I had left in September, waiting patiently, confident that I would come back alone, biding his time, like a spider weaving its web knowing for certain that the fly would come and be trapped. He dropped into our conversation that the next day was his birthday, and that he would like to take me to dinner, as a celebration. I look back and wonder whether his birthday was the only reason for his wanting to celebrate. But whatever – I think we both knew that the situation had leaped beyond control that first time our eyes met, the previous summer.

The next two weeks passed all too quickly, a heady mixture of abandonment, of total freedom, of fun and laughter, of being the sole attention of another person. And stupidly, carelessly, I fell under his spell. I didn't love him, I am sure. I don't even think that it was a need within me to have a man in my life. But he had made me happier than I had been in years, and I had become drunk on this joy, desperate to keep it, like an addict waiting for her next fix. I wanted time to stand still, to stay captured in that moment, like a snapshot. But the day came to return to England. Fritz drove me to the small airport in Gibraltar, helped me to check in and, after a tearful goodbye, watched me walk through to the departure lounge. We had made vague promises about the future. He knew that I was still working with Philip, and had tried to make me promise to stop, reasoning that Philip would control me, and try to force me to go back, that I would lose my newfound freedom. Unable to detect the fault lines in his logic, I did not recognise it for what it was: another man controlling my life, and that in fact I had already lost my freedom. My feelings for Philip were still in turmoil: I did not hate him, I had just stopped loving him, but I felt a loyalty to our business. I explained to Fritz that I needed to work, to earn a living, but I promised that I would expedite a financial settlement and somehow try to run my share of the business commuting between Spain and England so that he and I could spend time together in Spain.

February passed quickly in a flurry of arguments with Philip, solicitors' meetings, and hurried, difficult telephone calls from Fritz in Spain. He insisted on using a call box, so our calls were necessarily brief. Granted he was calm and comforting, advising me on how to handle the meetings, but he was also persistently demanding that I stop going to the office, stop seeing Philip. I remember when, trying to impart to him the importance of resolving the situation, I told him the sums of money involved and he had gasped and then laughed. Perhaps he could not believe his luck. Had he glimpsed a financially secure future for himself, a future that he felt was in danger of slipping out of his control the more I was away from him? I viewed his controlling interference as caring involvement. By this stage Philip knew that I was seeing Fritz; I think a 'friend' from Spain had telephoned him with the news, and understandably, this fuelled his anger at losing me. He probably had serious concerns that a share of our business might end up in Fritz's hands. But, finally, mutually agreed documents were ready to sign, and I planned my return to Spain.

I would have been happy to fly back to Spain, but the decision had been made at some point in our telephone conversations that I should take my car. Fritz flew to England the day before I was due to sign the papers. Our intention was to load my car with personal belongings and drive back to Spain via Holland, allowing time for him to visit some old friends. Perhaps he wanted to make sure that I really did leave England, and that by bringing my car, and most of my clothes I would begin to consider Spain as my new home. We were due to catch a ferry in the evening, but earlier that afternoon, Philip's solicitor called to say that he was not happy with the documents and would not allow Philip to sign them. I was devastated. Weeks of argument and discussion during which I felt that I had given as much as I could afford were thrown away in a moment.

Fritz stormed around the flat, cursing Philip. In tears, and desperate to resolve the matter, I telephoned our accountant who had been the architect of the agreement. He reassured me that he would sort things out and fax documents to me as soon as possible in Spain. Eventually we were able to leave, a little fraught, but in time for our ferry. I felt immensely sad at leaving England and Kate. Especially Kate. As she had spent half term with me, I would not be seeing her until the Easter holiday, so we had arranged for her to fly out to Spain to stay with me in the apartment, but I hated leaving her behind in England.

We arrived in The Hague, later that night. Fritz put a great deal of effort into showing me his home country and I greatly enjoyed our stay in Holland. From there we had a wonderful journey driving down to Spain. Fritz was very knowledgeable about Europe and spoke five languages fluently. We chose a slow meandering route and he took me to art galleries, museums, churches, little back street cafes and restaurants. We stayed in country villages and chateaux. We picnicked on fresh goats cheese bought from local farms, French bread and wine. I was permanently in awe of him, and gradually he took control. Slowly but surely I found myself handing over to him the reins of that freedom that I had so cherished when I had first left Philip. If I noticed the subtle changes I ignored them. I was enjoying myself too much. Fritz became the source of all my happiness

In Spain life settled into a blissful routine. Lazy days on the boat or around the port, evenings we dined more often now in local Spanish restaurants, a new experience for me. We would share our nights between the boat and the apartment. But this idyllic lifestyle was to be all too short-lived.

Occasionally Philip and I needed to speak about business and this quickly became a source of great irritation to Fritz. The strong and often crude language he used when referring to Philip was hurtful so I became secretive about these contacts. I felt guilty, keeping things from him, but did not have the ability to stand up to him. John was right in his instinct that I still had a long road to travel.

Though my old friends in the port did not actually avoid me, I had noticed that a coolness had begun to develop, and I became aware that nobody, nobody at all, seemed to like Fritz. He criticized everyone; a trait in him that I had not previously noticed, but which I found embarrassing, particularly as, in my opinion, his criticisms were more often than not unfounded. In particular his attacks were directed at those people whom I had known as friends. I had a growing feeling that he wanted to separate me from them completely. But I accepted this, convincing myself that I did not need them; that he was all I needed. So I was cut off from my friends in England, and was gradually losing contact with my friends in Spain.

I was looking forward immensely to seeing Kate at Easter, and though I understood that it would be difficult for her seeing me with another man so soon after leaving her father, I buried my concerns under my excitement. In an effort to stimulate her interest in Spain, something that she could look forward to on future visits, I had arranged for her to learn to ride at a local riding school that was run by an English girl. Kate learned very quickly, and thoroughly enjoyed her riding lessons. It very soon became clear that, despite his efforts to get along with her, Kate did not like Fritz. But it was wonderful to have her with me, even though I was continually walking a tightrope between my desire to be with her, and Fritz's demands on my attention.

All too soon the time came for her to return to England. Even though I would be flying back to see her three weeks later, the heartache on the journey to the airport was indescribable. We checked her in, and I waited to the last minute to allow her to leave me and walk through to the departure lounge. Almost blinded by tears, I ran up to the open deck, and watched her walk out and board the plane. As the plane taxied along the short runway I stretched out my arms, waving, hoping that she could see me through the tiny window, and I lifted that plane with my hands and my heart, sobbing uncontrollably, wanting desperately to reach out into space and hold her to me once more. I tore downstairs and out through the busy concourse, and ran the whole length of the main street as the plane took its graceful curving turn to set course for England; crying, sobbing, my heart breaking because I had just said goodbye to the person that I loved most in all the world.

For the remainder of that day, and the next, I was inconsolable. Fritz became exasperated and angry. He could not understand my inability to let Kate go. I think he realised then that he was in a battle for my love, not against another man, but against a child. Childless himself, he could never know, never understand that he was doomed to lose this battle. He had told me little of his childhood, except that, as the youngest and only boy his mother had adored him, and that one day when he was still very young, he had waved happily as she rode off in a car, driven by his father. He never saw her again. There had been a terrible accident in which she was killed, and his father so badly injured that he was in hospital for months. Fritz had not been allowed to attend the funeral and so had never had the opportunity to say goodbye to his mother. From that time on his father had remained distant from him, though materially Fritz received everything he could wish for.

CHAPTER 19

Fritz disliked men and shied away from any confrontation. Whilst psychologically powerful, he suffered from a muscular disease which caused him to limp slightly, and his movements were somewhat hampered by stiffness. Once, when we were walking up Gibraltar Main Street, we had to step sideways to avoid a ladder that was being used by decorators. As Fritz stepped around the ladder, he turned back to speak to me. At the same time, two men emerged from the building and he bumped into one of them.

"Out of my way you fucking Jew!" the man shouted.

I was deeply shocked, and angry. I had little or no personal experience of anti-Semitism only having heard of, or read accounts of the Nazi internment camps and the Russian pogroms. I looked at Fritz, expecting a furious riposte, but he did nothing. I turned away from him, arm extending to grab the man by the sleeve and demand an apology. But Fritz stopped me, "No, let it go!" He took my arm and pulled me away. Once clear of them he explained that he could not get into a fight; his disability would make him a sitting duck for a punch, which would knock him to the ground – even more humiliating than accepting the insult. This incident remained etched on my mind for days. For a man to be unable to physically stand up for himself must be an almost intolerable burden. Not only had his mother left him to fend for himself, he had inherited her Jewish blood and dark looks, as well as a disease that prevented him from defending himself in the way that would be instinctive for most men. The hand that he had been dealt could explain his overriding need for control. Unable to dominate physically, he had become a master of control, through his chosen profession.

Fritz was passionate about his boat, a huge two-masted schooner he had built with his wife's support. They had sailed it from Holland to the Mediterranean during the last few months of her life when she had been in the terminal stages of breast cancer. How had she coped with the confines of living on that boat, climbing up and down the galley stairs from deck to inside cabins? She must have been an incredibly strong woman, giving Fritz the final days and hours of her life, the joy of sailing his yacht on the first stage of their journey around the world. The schooner was designed for long term living with an exceptional amount of storage, galley, dining area, and two large sleeping cabins. Entertainment was not a problem; there was a TV, video recorder and stereo system; they had spent hours recording tapes from Meat Loaf to Beethoven, and there was a formidable library of books, mostly in Dutch. Fritz had not sailed since she died, and so that summer he began to talk about us taking the boat out, suggesting that we travel along the coast and across to Morocco. He even talked about the possibility of together continuing the dream journey around the world that he had planned with his wife. I did agree to a trip across the Straits to Morocco, confident that we could manage it between us, even if we motored most of the way, which in the event we did, but I was non-committal about the longer trip.

It was not until we left the marina for this first short trip along the coast that I realised his lack of confidence in managing the boat, especially when mooring alongside. He would scream instructions, and I did not take well to being shouted at, especially as I had sailed before and had a pretty good idea of what I was meant to be doing. Needless to say it was not a relaxing outing, and I decided that any long-term partnership as captain and crew was doomed. Perhaps his wife had been better able to ignore him. I made vague excuses for not making definitive plans for a long trip, citing my work and Kate as reasons for being unable to stray too far for too long. I knew that I could not be cooped up on the boat with him for weeks, possibly months on end.

The boat was his domain and he was possessive of everything in it. I had learnt that I dared not even touch or move certain items that were for him a strong tie to his wife.

I became less happy being on the boat, preferring my apartment where I felt comfortable amongst my own possessions. Unfortunately, Fritz felt familiar enough there to break china, glasses or spill red wine on my rugs with impunity.

Money soon became a major issue in our relationship. He owned his boat, but had no income other than a small annuity from a Dutch investment, and whatever he could earn tracing stolen yachts for an English insurer. I had more disposable income than he and always paid for our flights to and from the UK, as well as hotel bills when we were travelling. He began to complain that our extravagant lifestyle was bankrupting him. We set a limit on our weekly spending, but all this served to do was reinforce my growing realisation of our incompatibility.

So the summer months passed. A mix of time in Spain and short trips to England to spend exeat weekends or half term with Kate, interspersed with travelling through Europe on Fritz's various insurance trips, trawling along the coastlines, marina hopping, trying to trace stolen boats. I was not as happy as I had been. The reality of being so often and so long without Kate, and the guilt of leaving her was beginning to affect me deeply, and despite the sunshine I missed my home country more than I could have imagined. The more that Fritz sensed my longings for home and child, the more erratic his behaviour became.

As a psychologist, I believe that Fritz was easily able to encourage my dependency on him. He did this covertly, without immediate realisation on my part of the loss of my independence. By now he was automatically using and driving my car as if it were his own. I drove less and less, even the short trip down to the port. He had keys to my apartment, and he used my telephone and fax for international business calls, accusing me of being petty when I asked if he could reimburse me the sometimes very high costs of these calls.

He began to regale me with stories of previous lovers, in particular a German woman whom he had known some eighteen months earlier. I did not have the wit to wonder how he could tell me one minute that he was still desperately missing his wife, and the next enthuse about his recent conquests. He displayed an infatuation with a local doctor's wife; blonde and extremely attractive. I knew from confidences that she had shared with me that she was very unhappy in her marriage and had already embarked on one affair, and so I began to feel very insecure. On one occasion Fritz insisted that we invite her and her husband to dinner in the apartment. I suffered his attentions to her the whole evening but when they left I accused him of betraying my feelings. The flaming row that followed was dreadful. He screamed at me, stamping around the apartment, flinging accusations at me of being hard and uncaring, and of pushing him towards her. He stormed out slamming the door, leaving me cowering on the floor in tears, in a corner of the kitchen. Eventually I went to bed miserable and lonely, but nevertheless realising that somehow I had to end this stormy relationship. The following morning, I walked down to the marina, and along the far pontoon towards his boat, having summoned the courage to ask for my keys back. He was standing on the foredeck and watched me walk towards him. He pre-empted all that I had been going to say to him, calmed me, held me, convinced me that it was I that had been unreasonable and that he loved me and we should be together. And I believed him.

Fritz could recall very little of the short relationship he had with his mother. It had been his older sister who had told him what little he knew, and of how much his mother had adored him. I believed that he still harboured strong feelings for his mother, and deep, unexpressed sadness at not being allowed to say goodbye. On one of our trips through Holland he had taken a detour to a cemetery, not telling me why, and I had held back as he approached a large headstone. I waited and watched. It was a still, cloudy day and had been raining on and off, the only sound now being the quiet drip of rain through the trees. We were the only people present and I heard him say;

"Mama, mama, why did you leave me?"

Why did he speak the words in English and not his native Dutch? Were they meant for me to hear? Was he asking me to make up for the loss of his mother? Was I supposed to love him unconditionally, accepting his ill temper and faults as a mother would accept those of an adored child? I could never work out whether he was angry with my inability to give him the love he wanted, or with her for abandoning him.

I knew by the end of that summer of 1994 that the relationship could not last, yet still I could not push him away. He had gradually taken control of every aspect of my life, playing with me like a yo-yo. One minute he was adoring and holding and loving me, the next pushing me away, accusing me of every imaginable fault and failing. But after each push away, when the cord with which he held me had reached the limit of its arc, with no place further to go, I would make the inevitable return to his hand. I became fearful of his every reaction to anything that I might say or do, my confidence drained like the bathwater through an open plughole. I was trapped. That brief period of independence that I had experienced when I left Philip was but a memory. How is it that I could walk out on my husband of twenty-five years, but not leave this man whom I had known only several months, of which only the first two or three had been happy? I believe the answer lies in the lesson of my childhood, learned from the first man that I loved. To receive love I had to deny my own wishes, and succumb to demands that I did not like. I had not been taught that it was only right and natural that I should express my own wishes and needs within the relationship of a man and a woman. If I wanted to be loved I had to accept being abused. And Fritz, as a trained psychologist would know this.

THE CANDLE

Am I an object of men's desire?
To be used at a whim
To give pleasure
And to be grateful for the short time of love shown

What else am I here for?

To be myself?
To have my own thoughts and desires?
To colour and shape the pattern of my own life?

No

My body is not mine, but theirs to use
To fuck
To gratify their inherent need for power over woman

My mind is not mine, but theirs to control
To rape
To bend and shape to their will
To hold in their power

My thoughts of choice and freedom
To be crushed before revolt
Don't even try to fight
The war is lost even before the first battle fought

Is this my belief?

The inheritance I leave my daughter?
Can I not show her the power of a woman?
Can I not guide her to a better path?
Can I not lead her along a brighter road?

For it is there
I have no doubt

The path to fulfilment
That I could not travel

Lacking the strength of will to be my own self
Until it becomes too late
The passing of years
Slowly eroding the mountain of my desire
To forge my own life, to strike out for my own purpose
To say

No
I do not want this

I will fight to give my daughter the truth
I will give her a candle to hold up and say
This is my light
And I will not hide it or let it be smothered

For I am a woman
Therefore I am strong

I am a woman
And I will shape my own destiny

I am a woman
And I will forge my own future
And let no man, or his son, own me

I had yet to reach the same stage as I had with Philip, where I was able to make the choice between being alone and possibly unhappier, than being 'loved' but unhappy. But this time I was in a strange country, with no familiar places to hide, and believed that I had lost my friends. And this time, though I had not realised it, I was in battle with a more formidable opponent than Philip. Fritz knew how to play the game far better than I did; he knew how to control me through my weaknesses, he was the game master, and held all the aces.

But this time my subconscious did not wait for the conscious to make the decision. Eventually, pushed to the limits of endurance, Mother Nature took control and made the decision for me.

CHAPTER 20

Late summer 1994, with the fast approaching end of the first year's lease on the apartment that I had rented in Sunninghill, the idea of buying my own house in England began to firm. My strong homing instinct kicked in, and it became clear to me that the place where my heart rested was England; I needed to make a home for Kate and myself.

In an effort to keep the uneasy peace between us I explained to Fritz that it was simply the practicality of wanting and needing a base in England to spend quality time with Kate. Surprisingly, he fell in with my wishes. Yet this, too, soon erupted into rows, because I would start my conversation with the agents:

"I would like to buy..." rather than "We would like to buy..."

He had suggested that I should put the house in both our names for after all we were living together. But I was determined to be resolute in this matter and whilst I could not summon the courage to give him an outright "No", I avoided talking to him about it.

When I eventually found the right property, a pretty little village house in old Sunningdale – where Philip still lived in our old house – it was bought with my money and in my name alone. I knew that our relationship was doomed, and though I had not even begun to think how I was going to extricate myself, buying my own home in England was the first step towards this end.

After several visits to and from England during October and November of that year, we finally moved in on December 4th 1994. We had agreed to stay for Christmas, returning to Spain via Holland, in the New Year, when Kate had returned to school. Kate spent Christmas with us, and the boys came on Christmas morning with Mark, a close friend, to have breakfast and to exchange presents. Prior to this my sons had only met Fritz once, briefly, and both had taken a dislike to him. Adam in particular had always been protective of me, and would at that stage probably not have accepted that any man would have been suitable. Needless to say, though everyone tried, it was not the easiest of days, and I think that the boys were probably quietly incensed at the way Fritz behaved as though the house, the woman, and all in it were his property.

On New Year's Eve we had invited another couple to dinner. Karin, an old girlfriend of mine, had also left her husband and developed a relationship with an Italian, Alfredo. Fritz was absolutely charming, and Karin thought him delightful. Although I was somewhat tense because we had argued over the cooking and presentation of the meal, we had a lovely evening, and started 1995 on a happy note.

I was totally besotted with my new home, just being in it, cleaning it, and fussing with furniture and ornaments. But most of all it was wonderful to have somewhere that Kate and I could call our own. For the first time in my life I owned my own home and I cannot begin to describe how significant this was for me, and how strongly it impacted my emotional well-being. I could choose who came through the door. I could make decisions about what happened within those four walls. The security it represented for me was unparalleled. There was only one black cloud on the horizon, and as the clock ticked by into 1995 this cloud loomed larger and larger. The planned date for our departure for Spain drew near and my soul became heavy with dread. I knew I was allowing myself to be dragged along on a journey that I really did not wish to make, but yet again I put myself in denial of my own needs in order to bend to another person's will, falling into the ingrained pattern of being unable to say what I would prefer.

The journey to Holland passed relatively quietly. I was withdrawn and quiet, but Fritz probably assumed that my sadness was due to leaving Kate, which in part it was. We stayed in a motel near The Hague, from which each day he drove us to various old acquaintances and storage depots to collect personal belongings that he wished to take to Spain. The day we were due to leave, he packed the car to the hilt, using every conceivable space, ignoring my pleas to take care with the leather upholstery and roof lining, insisting that he knew best, demanding that I leave it to him.

Standing in the motel room, close to tears, the knowledge that I really did not want to go back to Spain with him grew stronger with each passing minute. Finally, summoning the courage from I know not where, I walked outside where he was struggling with a painting and told him. He did not make any attempts to persuade me to change my mind, but immediately flew into a rage. I had thought that he would adopt his cajoling, persuasive, "we need to be together" line, the one that I always found impossible to resist. I turned my back on him and walked into the motel room without a word. He followed, still ranting at me. Suddenly in mid-stream, he stopped and looked at me, going quiet, realisation dawning that I really meant what I was saying. The next ten minutes passed in a stream of muttered curses as he stamped back and forth from the car unpacking the contents. I was shocked, and a little apprehensive at this seemingly easy victory.

Finally I stood there, car keys once again in my own hand, ready to step in, take over my life and drive back to England. But I couldn't. At that final instant I could not walk away. I still loved him. Loved him, or needed him? I think I was in love with the idea of him, with what we had had in those first few weeks. I stood there staring at him, confused and frightened, thinking about coping with the long drive and ferry crossing alone. He looked at me quizzically, then he grinned, and I was lost. He must have been confident that by suddenly handing me back control I would be wrong-footed, unsure that I could actually manage without him. He had called my bluff and I had folded.

We drove quickly through Belgium and down into France, having planned to spend a night with Rick, an old friend of his, a retired policeman from the Kent constabulary. Rick had married a Frenchwoman, Jeanette, and was living in the Gironde area of France in an old French farmhouse. Though still quiet and pensive, after ten days in Holland surrounded by Dutch speaking people, I was delighted to meet an Englishman and enjoy the conversation and very

English humour, which we two shared. Fritz spoke fluent French with Jeanette, and the evening passed with much wine flowing, chatter and laughter. It wasn't until we went to bed that I discovered that once again, I had disappointed him.

In the privacy of our bedroom, he let loose with cold and quiet fury, accusing me of making passes at Rick, of being unfaithful, a whore, a selfish bitch, whatever. I had never seen him so angry. I cowered away from him, nowhere to run. Weeping uncontrollably, I let him continue, not shouting loudly – maybe aware that we could be overheard – but cursing me violently through tight lips. I slowly undressed and I lay in bed, shaking, watching him fume, leaning over me, almost spitting his fury into my face. Whilst his ranting had always been frightening, he had never hit me or attacked me physically. But this time he boiled over. By now undressed, he pulled the sheets back and fell over me, his knees either side of my quaking body, and for the first time, he assaulted me physically, pinned me to the bed and, ignoring my feeble struggles and refusal, raped me, each violent thrust accompanied by stinging verbal abuse. I fell into an exhausted sleep, but unbeknown to either of us, my body had been abused once too often, my mind cried "Enough", and when I awoke the next morning it was as though someone else was in control of my actions.

As we journeyed south I started to weep. Sitting in the passenger seat, unable to hold myself erect, I wept. Silently, profoundly, unremittingly wept. Through the afternoon across the Pyrenees, through the evening and the night, across Spain heading ever southwards I wept. The tears held in check for a lifetime, poured down my cheeks; would not, could not stop. Whilst he parked the car and unloaded the contents into the apartment, I sat and wept. Gently, perhaps aware that this time he had pushed me too far, perhaps also realising that this was different, dangerous, threatening his plans, he put me to bed, and left to spend the night on his boat. My tears soaked the pillow long before I finally slipped into an exhausted sleep.

I woke alone the next morning. The telephone was ringing on the bedside table next to me. I picked it up.

"How are you?" he asked.

Without thinking, without considering, the words came out,

"I want to go home."

"But you are home."

"No, I want to go home, back to England." And I hung up on him.

Within minutes he was there with me, cajoling, softly speaking, encouraging;

"Stay here, I can make you better. You'll be fine in a day or two."

"No, I want to go home."

Those five words were all I could say, all I kept repeating to him.

"I have to get home."

Sitting there on the bed, tear-stained face, yesterday's make-up in runnels down my cheeks, dishevelled hair; I must have looked a mess. I would not look at him, instead preferring to look at my hands clinging to the edge of the bed, or out of the large French window towards the open sea. I started rocking, slowly backwards and forwards.

"I want to go home."

Why he relented, I do not know, but he had me booked on a flight back to London that evening. He drove me to Malaga airport, and we spent a miserable hour waiting for my departure. I had insisted on bringing my case full of clothes, still unpacked from our journey down, and perhaps he sensed that maybe this was our end. He resorted to tears over a cup of airport coffee, telling me that he was worried about me, that he was scared that he might never see me again. Was this a double bluff? Was he subliminally threatening me with what he thought and hoped – that I feared I might never see him again? In a perverse way his tears gave me strength and added to my determination. Tearfully but resolutely I boarded my flight, not fully understanding what was behind the need to go home. But, like an animal that is mortally wounded, instinct was calling me back to my lair and familiar territory.

I have no memory of that flight, or the journey to my home. Once there I fell into a deep sleep, and woke late the next morning. I passed the day aimlessly wandering around the house, alternately making coffee and weeping, unable to focus on anything. At some stage I telephoned John, whom I had not seen for eighteen months. I told him that there was something wrong, that I didn't understand why but I could not stop crying, and that I felt very, very tired. He told me to come to his house the following morning.

John took one look at me and must have realised that there was indeed something wrong. By the time I saw him, I had been crying almost non-stop for four days. He showed me up the narrow staircase to his small consulting room on the left at the top, and gently sat me down on the sofa. He sat opposite me and asked how I was. I started to talk, but my mouth refused to form the words. An immeasurable tiredness overcame me, and, perhaps sensing that here at last was a safe place to let go, all command slipped away. My limbs felt weak and my spine no longer stiff enough to support me. I folded over and slid onto the floor, not quite unconscious, but as though drugged, my mind either unable or unwilling even to take control of my body anymore. I lay there, dimly aware of John calling for his wife, who was a nurse.

A flurry of activity carried on over my head as John and Jo made arrangements for me to be taken into hospital. Snatches of their conversation drifted into my brain, registered, but received no response. I lay on the floor; my exhausted, damaged mind relieved to switch off and release all the decision making to someone else. When the time came to leave, I was barely able to move. John and Jo struggled to get me downstairs to the car, my legs dragging beneath me as though they belonged to a marionette, the strings either not connected, or held still by the puppeteer. I could not make them move one before the other to walk. I fell onto the back seat of the car, and lay there, speechless, thoughtless, sliding like a tied bundle of rags from side to side with the motion of the car as it took the turns and twists to the place where I would spend the next two months of my life.

THE TREE

A sapling
A young tree
Newly shot through the earth
To bloom and grow
Green stick
Flexible
Weak, shallow roots
Quivers and bends in the wind
Leaves fluttering in joyful abandon

Unknowing and so
Unafraid
Of the power of its adversary
Defiant in its innocence
Each storm a fresh challenge

Blow me
Shake me
Bend me
What can you do?
That I cannot thrive

Years pass
The tree forms
Branches, trunk, body and soul
Set in their stance
Against the winds of the storms

Their greenness gone
Turned in time
To hard, dark, unbending
Fixed, rigid
Branches, extending
Bearing too much

Their defiance turned to acceptance

The wind will win
Patiently
Biding its time
Until
With one last puff
Breaks the over-laden tree
No longer able to bend and bow

Tearing limb from trunk
Straining against its deep-set roots
The tree falls
Crashing to the ground
A death's roar of sound

No more vibrant
Swaying to the tune of life

It lies
Still and quiet
Waiting
While the wind dances away

It will not stand again
So strong and proud
It will not quiver again nor bend
With the blowing winds

Laying still on the forest floor
Waiting

Who will come?

Who will look and see?
The potential
Of a new life
Or an end to the old

Its last gift to this world
Through the warm embers of a fire
Bestowing upon others
What it could not hold for itself

Or taken and carved
Through imaginative eyes and mind
A new life
Tenderly, lovingly
Encouraged, shaped and refined
Beautiful
Admired
Firm and strong

No longer subject
To the vagaries of the winds
It will live on
In the eyes of those who view
The metamorphosis completed.

CHAPTER 21

January 25th, 1995, the day that I entered the clinic. I vaguely remember being half dragged, half carried into the entrance lobby, a spacious room with polished wooden floors, beautiful flower arrangements and comfy sofas along one wall. I had nightclothes and a wash bag, so we must have stopped off at home to collect them. I remember sitting in a bed, in a darkened room, being questioned by a man who I would learn was to be in charge of my psychiatric care for the duration of my stay. I had no idea who he was, but he carried an air of authority, and appeared angry with me. His questions were harsh, and I felt that he was trying to demonstrate that I was pretending to be ill, and that I was actually quite capable of getting up, dressed and taking myself off home. I tried not to cry, tried to answer him honestly, thinking that maybe I should just try and pull myself together. Suddenly he stood, patted my arm gently and left the room.

I have no recollection of anything more until some few days later I awoke to see Michael, the vicar from our local church, standing over me quietly praying. I had no sense of the time that had passed, and the first thought that entered my head was that I was dying and Michael had been called to pray for me. My eyes flicked around the room. Was it a different one? Had I gone to sleep in one bed and woken in another? They rested on Michael, who looked at me kindly and asked how I was feeling.

"I'm tired."

He told me that I had slept for five days.

My next visitor was the psychiatrist; I shall call him Maurice, who had seemed so unfriendly the last time we met. He was a handsome man, tall, grey hair, slightly receding, and had an air of authority that was intimidating. I sat up, and looked at him nervously, expecting another tirade. But he was much different this time. Speaking softly, he apologised for upsetting me, and told me that it had been necessary, in order for him to confirm how ill I was. He told me that I would be staying for a while, that he would prescribe some drugs to help me feel better, and that I should be seeing him once a week. He also said that, in addition to seeing him, I would need to talk to a psychotherapist. I wanted desperately to see John, dear John, who had brought me to the clinic, someone whom I knew, and could trust. In the event John came to see me, and agreed for the immediate future to visit me once a week.

The clinic, set in lovely gardens, was a converted country house; extended to add an indoor swimming pool, exercise and therapy rooms. There were some fifteen bedrooms varying in size and comfort, all en-suite, the patients coming from all over the country. Some were recovering alcoholics, and readily said as much, but generally there was an unwritten understanding that unless details were offered, one did not ask why people were staying. Perhaps many did not even know the answer themselves. Each of us living in our own world, developed with a protective outer shell, a barrier both to prevent inward incursion of hurtful words or actions, and outward seepage of emotions or feelings that would make the world within vulnerable to attack. Body language gave out the message – do not disturb.

Breakfast was always served in our bedrooms, giving us an opportunity to prepare for the day, and meet other people, in our own time. We were discouraged from staying in our rooms after breakfast though, and were expected to attend the structured daily program. Exercise classes were on offer most mornings before coffee, and in the afternoon a group therapy session, which was pretty much compulsory, was held in the large lounge. This would be followed by yoga or some form of relaxation class. The lounge was an oddly shaped room, but open and large. In one corner, opposite to the entrance door, was a rarely used television set, and along one wall a large recessed window looked out onto the front driveway, which was surrounded by flowerbeds. The main feature of the lounge, and for me the most attractive, was a large wood-burning stove that had two comfortable armchairs, either side of it. My second favourite place in the house, after my bedroom, was one of these chairs, and I was most often to be found curled up in one of them, my feet tucked up under my bottom, hands firmly closed around a mug of hot chocolate, staring into the fire, or reading a book. The mug of hot chocolate was my standby, my only source of food on the days when I refused to eat or could not face sitting at the table with the others.

Lunch and evening dinner were served in the dining area off the main lobby, where we all sat around a long oak refectory table. The food was exquisite, beautifully prepared and served; two courses for lunch and three for dinner. Like the classes, meals were not to be missed unless exceptional circumstances prevailed. The staff, apart from the domestics, kitchen and cleaners, were all ex-nurses who had re-trained in mental health care, and I came to learn that many of them had their own experience of emotional suffering.

Nobody that I have asked can recollect how word got about that I was back in England and in a clinic. But it did, to the extent that as the days and weeks passed I became greatly touched by the love and caring shown by friends and acquaintances alike. My room looked like a flower shop, and there were cards on every surface. Michael, the vicar, was a regular visitor, and I have been told that he strictly controlled all other visitors from the church, which was probably just as well, because I was not too communicative and very tired. Anne visited often and took charge of my washing. She tells me that she now has an intense dislike of the clinic, and most particularly the perfume that I wore at the time, associating it with my ill health. Kate's first knowledge of my illness was when Adam collected her from the school bus on the Friday evening of her weekend exeat. She says that as soon as she saw him waiting there instead of me she knew something was wrong. Philip knew of course, and would bring Kate to visit me whenever he could. I guess that he may have been the first person that John called, as he would have been the only contact number for me that John would have had. Aaron was living and studying in Reading at the time, but came very often to see me, usually evenings. And then there was one other visitor.

How he knew where I was I have no idea, but Fritz flew over from Spain within the first few days, and settled himself into my house. I have very little memory of his visits to the clinic and what was said. At that stage I was still sleeping most of the time, and confined to my room. Michael has since told me that on one occasion Fritz asked him to persuade me to check myself out and go back to Spain with him. Like my friends in Spain, nobody in England liked Fritz, and Michael with his protective, caring instinct refused to be cajoled into doing something that he believed would not be right for me. Anne tells me that one evening she was standing outside my room with Fritz, when he remarked that I was too close to my children. "I soon put him right on that one," was her comment.

One day, Maurice came into my room and without preamble told me that I needed either to '...send that man back to Spain' or check out. Horrified, I asked why. His reply was to the effect that Fritz was undoing all the good that the staff and doctors were trying to do for me and that I may as well go stay in a five star hotel. Petrified of the reaction from Fritz, and yet just as unable to contemplate leaving this safe haven, I asked Maurice if he would talk to Fritz, knowing that there would be the most awful row if I tried to tell him that he had to return to Spain. He refused point blank, explaining that it was time for me to stand up for myself and take control of my life. My mind was in a whirl. I felt safe in the clinic, safer than I had in a long time. I was cared for; nothing to do at that stage, except sleep and eat, and I knew that I could not return to the lifestyle that had recently ended so dramatically. But even so, for a brief instant, I did wonder if I could recover just as well if I went to an hotel, believing that all I needed was rest and good food. I still had absolutely no idea of the tumultuous journey that I was about to undertake.

Anguishing over the choice, I asked Maurice if maybe Fritz could just visit me less often.

"No."

So, tentatively I agreed, but asked if I could do it by telephone – less confrontational.

Maurice replied that he didn't mind how I did it, as long as I did, and soon. When Fritz left after his afternoon visit, I allowed enough time for him to return to the house and then called. I was sitting on a chair in the entrance lobby, dreading the conversation that I was about to instigate, the telephone shaking in my hand. I told Fritz that it might be better if he returned to Spain, to wait for me there, that the doctors had said that I would get better more quickly if he was not around. His anger erupted, I guess at the control being taken out of his hands once again, as well as the implied insult. A torrent of furious abuse poured down the telephone line at me. I cried out, a broken heart-rending cry, unable to respond with any coherent language; it was as if his words were a stick, beating me.

The telephone fell to the floor, and I followed it, slipping from the chair, shaking uncontrollably, sobbing, wanting to shut down and go to sleep, to slip quickly into the darkness away from all this hurt. The remaining clear image I have was of Anne's horrified face as she appeared around the corner from the entrance hall, her eyes taking in the scene. Behind her was Aaron.

The nurses gathered round, gently picking me up, telling me how proud they were, how strong I had been, what a clever girl I was. I now know that they had been fore-warned, that this was the first test of my journey. A seminal moment, but it did not feel like that to me. I was too distressed to understand the implications of what I had just done. Back to my room, I was given more drugs to help my mind to shelter from the storm, in blissful sleep once again; a healing sleep in which my subconscious would start to sift through the mess of my emotions and begin to put into place, the first tiny brick of the foundation of my road to healing. But the journey down was far from over. I had yet to reach rock bottom.

Aaron took matters into his own hands, enlisting his brother in the 'eviction', both of them finally able to release their anger at Fritz without risk of upsetting me. They drove to my house and 'suggested' that Fritz pack his bags and get on the next flight back to Spain. I am told that he needed a 'helping hand' with his packing, and that they made sure that he arrived at Heathrow in plenty of time for his flight, which he had paid for with my credit card. Had he made a note of the number? Anxieties surfaced the following day when I had had time to think about the practical implications, worrying about how he might express his anger. He still had keys to my apartment, and my car in Spain. But the boys promised to take care of everything. Within twenty-four hours the locks on the apartment had been changed, and a friend had been contacted and agreed to drive my car over to England for me.

CHAPTER 22

I had never recovered the weight that I lost during the time of my perceived food sensitivity when I was still married to Philip and weighed a little over 8st when I was taken into the clinic. To put this into perspective, I now weigh around 9st 12lb and most people reckon I am slim. Once I had passed that initial period of staying in my room and sleeping most of the time, the nurses began to insist that I join the group for meals at the refectory table and try to eat more.

This was a struggle for me. I was happy with my weight, felt strong enough, and in any case did not have much of an appetite. Furthermore, I was nervous of conversation, and I viewed all the new faces at the table as unfriendly and unwilling for me to join what I perceived as their select group. I was a newcomer and they had already formed their small breakaway factions that conferred, shared secrets and laughed at private jokes, compounding my feelings of being unwanted, and unlikeable.

It was far too soon, and I far too inexperienced in the ways of institutions to understand that each and every one had felt the same as me until they had latched onto another hurting soul for comfort and companionship. I had to find my own relationships, not intrude upon theirs. Besides, my arrival had been rather dramatic, I had been confined to my room for over a week, and some had seen the episode at the telephone. So I was probably regarded as a bit of an oddity, a fresh subject for gossip. My body language was closed, and those who would have been more naturally inclined to chat were probably unsure of how to approach me, or to open a conversation. Consequentially my first few mealtimes 'en famille' were excruciatingly uncomfortable. I would sit there, shoulders hunched and curved around, eyes lowered, to convey my wish to be left alone.

SOUP

Sitting at the long table
Seemingly disappearing into the distance
At either side of her
Unfriendly faces opposite
Neighbours chatting
Not to her

She picks up the napkin
Beautifully folded beside her place setting
Slowly with deliberate movements
Unfolds each carefully pressed line
Smoothing it onto her lap
Actions taken with calculated decision
To occupy her thoughts
Closed from those around

The bowl of soup
Placed before her
Smells good
She picks up the spoon
The correct one?
Yes
Round not oval
Dipping into the hot soup
Front to back
Collecting the delicious creamy mix
Of vegetables and meat

Lifting the spoon to her mouth
Her hand is shaking
She bends forward
Over the bowl
And the table

The soup, so lovingly prepared
Now erratically shaken
Falls downward
In large globules
Over the bowl
And the table

Eyes flicker up and around
Briefly checking the company
Did anyone see?
No
Is anyone watching?
No

Safe from scrutiny
She dips again
The spoon
Into the bowl
Front to back
Collecting again the creamy delicious mix
Of vegetables and meat
Her hand still shaking
The spoon arrives
Once again
Empty

Maybe not the soup
Not hungry anyway
Head down
One tear
Drops
Over the bowl
And the table

Enclosed in this world of shame
She senses rather than feels
Someone behind her
Two large, black, hands appear

Either side, over her shoulders
Stopping for an instant
To gently squeeze
Encouragement

Taking her small, white, shaking hands
In his
Holding the bowl with one
The spoon firmly in the other
Dips
Into the bowl
Front to back
Collecting again the creamy blend
Of vegetables and meat

Together
Lifting the spoon to her mouth
She sups
The warmth
Filling her mouth and stomach
The warmth
Of his hands around hers
Continues
Until
The bowl is empty

A whispered
"Well done"
Is all that passes
In recognition
Of their joint effort

The tears this time
Flooding
Softly downward
Over the bowl
And table

My feeding became a constant battle with the nurses, exacerbated by those mealtimes when I refused even to come to the table. I simply did not want to eat. My lack of interest in food must have been reported to Maurice, because in our subsequent meeting he broached the subject. Luckily, he was not concerned that I may become anorexic, and we made a pact that provided my weight stayed the same I could eat as and when I felt able, but if I chose to miss a meal I should take a cup of hot chocolate – obviously he was also aware that this had become my comforter. And I accepted that the scales would be brought to my room once a week for my weight to be monitored.

On Monday, Wednesday and Friday morning, shortly after breakfast, an aerobics class was held in the newly developed, underground hall. I had always enjoyed aerobics, going to classes once or twice a week for several years until I met Fritz. After breakfast the cleaning ladies came to our rooms to make beds and tidy the bathroom, though I always had the bed made before they arrived. They were busy and chatty, and very friendly, but I was more inclined to leave them to it, not even wanting to make the effort that light inconsequential conversation required. The aerobics classes were therefore an easy and inviting option for me to kill an hour or so before morning coffee.

Music has always been a source of great enjoyment for me, and like many people there have been particular pieces of music that I associate with special moments in my life. At times when I have been lonely or low, times when I have been ecstatically happy, and when I have been in love, there has always been a special song or piece of music that has become my passion, through which my feelings have soared or dived according to the mood. Love songs, classical music, passionate and exciting or soulful and heartrending, all providing a place to lose myself and express my emotions, releasing frustrated feelings, or fulfilling my desire for excitement.

When my marriage to Philip was breaking down many of my favourites were by Queen – '*I Want To Break Free*', '*It's A*

Kind Of Magic', *'Breakthru'*, *'Who Wants To Live Forever'*. Corny perhaps, but at the time very relevant and meaningful.

I cannot sit still when listening to passionate music, and I love dancing, though I have never had formal lessons.

Fritz introduced me to Rachmaninov, and to this day the piece of music that I love most of all is the piano concerto no 2. But the love song that we shared, that meant so much to us at the beginning of our relationship when we were unsure if we would be able to be together, was *'I Will Always Love You'*, sung by Whitney Houston. It was and probably always will be 'our song' and it is only fairly recently that I have become able to listen to it without shedding a tear.

The aerobics teacher used a great many popular songs for our workout, and she had included this song after the warm up programme for the slow stretching. I clung desperately to reality, the here and now, as it played seemingly interminably whilst we slowly extended and stretched arms then legs; tears rolling down my cheeks, fighting to keep control, focusing on my body feelings not my overpowering emotions. If she was aware of my distress, the teacher ignored it. She had to keep the class running, and maybe I had to learn that this is how it would be. To accept that life would throw up shocks, blasts from the past, and I would have to get on and get over them. So I struggled through. On subsequent days I knew it was coming, for she used the same tape.

Valentine's day, February 14th 1995, and as I came downstairs after breakfast to attend the class, I was called to reception. Some flowers had arrived for me – two-dozen beautiful red roses. I was excited, wondering, 'Who has sent them.' Was I being optimistically romantic, or just plain stupid? I read the label attached to them – 'Love Fritz'. Those two little words from my Svengali, drawing me back to him with a gift, a love offering. Still holding the yoyo and reeling me back in. Dumbfounded, not knowing which way I wanted to run; back to him, or forward away from him, I looked up at the nurse. Her eyes spoke volumes. Knowing whom the flowers were from and probably what I was feeling she asked if

I wanted them in my room. I could sense the answer she was looking for, and I gave it – vehemently:

"No, definitely not."

It would be like having his presence hovering, his shadow falling across me, smothering my attempts at becoming independent. This was why he had sent them! I wanted to smash them, tear them to pieces, and take out all my anger on those beautiful red roses. The man was not there, the flowers were, and they were a safe alternative on which to vent my anger. But I couldn't. Like the time at the motel in Holland; yet again I was drawn back to him, not far enough travelled along the road away to be able to resist the magnetic pull. The nurse read my face, watched these conflicting emotions flicker across them like a silent movie.

"What shall I do with them?" she asked softly.

"I don't know, whatever, I really don't know…"

My voice trailed away and I turned and walked along the corridor to the stairs leading down to the exercise hall, leaving her standing there with the roses. Like an automaton, I prepared for the class, my emotions raging, running between anger and grief.

The music started, something fast to warm us up, and then the slow stretch, our song "*I Will Always Love You*". The reminder, the magnetic pull exerting its force even in here. I stood upright, my mind screaming like a banshee, the inside of my head torn apart by the spinning tornado of emotional debris. Looking desperately for a way out, a way to end this turmoil of love and anger, hurt and deep despair, I ran across the room pushing other women out of my way, blindly heading for the door, the staircase, the corridor, outside and along the drive, running, stumbling, trying to escape the dreadful demons in my head who were re-igniting their smouldering black fires of stinking, rotting rubbish, starting new conflagrations with the fuel of recently abused love, poked and prodded with stabbing forks of pain. Will they never be allowed to die out?

THE GINGERBREAD MAN

You can run and run
As fast as you can
You can't catch me
I'm a gingerbread man

Children's rhyme
Over and over
Round and through

You can run and run
As fast as you can
You can't escape me
You can't escape you

Evil little man
Frightening, persistent
Demon she knew

Run and run
You can't escape me
You can't escape you

Branches of trees
Joining the race
Tearing her arms
Scratching her face

Run and run
As far as you can
You can't escape me
You can't escape you

The beat of the rhythm
Matching her feet
Pounding and pounding

Out to the street

Jump, jump
As far as you can
You can't escape me
You can't escape you

The scream of the brakes
The slam of a door
A voice in her ear
Why this?
What for?

Run and run
As fast as you can
You can't escape me
You can't escape you

The voice from afar
Softly speaks

And somehow the calm
Of its words seeps through
The pounding rhythm
The fabric of pain

On and on
Over again

Run and run
As fast as you can
You can't escape me
You can't escape you

"Listen here
To me"
They softly implore

"Listen here
Stay and fight
Don't run anymore

You must
You can
Beat the gingerbread man"

I stumbled along the driveway, desperate to stop this unceasing torture. Emotional pain cannot be healed with an antiseptic wipe and a band-aid, or a codeine tablet. The only relief would be through oblivion, obtainable through sleep, even drug-induced sleep. Waking it is ever present. Conscious life becomes unbearable, unliveable, a long extended vista, stretching into forever, a landscape of swirling mists of pain and indescribable sadness.

Turning off the drive I ran into a large, overhanging, evergreen shrub, pushing the branches away, lashing out, scratching my arms and hands, but nonetheless hitting back at something. Sobbing I cried out to the heavens, to God,

"I can't do this anymore!"

And with shocking clarity I knew that I couldn't. Couldn't live anymore. Life was too painful, too full of sadness.

At the end of the drive the road curved gently around disappearing in both directions. Standing there, waiting for the sound of an approaching vehicle, I knew this was going to hurt. But still, then it would be over. No more hurt. I held no thoughts of consequences or anyone else, nothing except a desire to end this difficult, agonizing life.

A lorry came hurtling around the bend to my right, and was past me in a flash. Too late; I could not wait for the sound of an approaching vehicle. I stepped off the kerb into the middle of the road and lay down, calmly waiting, the hard gravelly surface scraping my arms and legs. I closed my eyes, and waited for the peace that would surely come.

Seconds, a minute, I don't know how long I lay there. But the inevitable squeal of brakes came. The car not quite moving fast enough for me, or maybe the driver moved his foot too fast onto the brake pedal. Two feet appeared by my head. I curled myself into a tight ball, foetal position, wanting not to be here, not through embarrassment but because I did not want to be here anymore. A man's voice, a cockney accent:

"It can't be that bad love."

Joined by a woman's:

"She must be from that place next door."

The man bent down and touched me, lightly, kindly. Before he could speak again, a nurse from the clinic appeared at his shoulder and took over, and then another, between them lifting me to my feet. Unable, unwilling to walk, they were forced to half carry, half drag me back into the clinic, to my bedroom. There they left me alone, perhaps to consider the gravity of what I had done. No judgement, no words of comfort, but neither were there words of condemnation. Not yet.

I tried again, was it later that day, or the next? I don't recall. But such was my determination. I failed again. This time they caught me as I reached the end of the drive. Had they been watching, to see if I was really suicidal or just crying out for attention? I did not want attention. Attention would not cure me. Attention would not sort out my tormented mind.

This time the nurse stayed with me, calmed me, but giving no indication of compassion or sorrow. Eventually she told me in a firm, but kind voice, what I could not refuse to acknowledge, but what I did not want to hear:

"If you succeed in killing yourself, I can promise you, guarantee, that at least one of your children will end up in a place like this! Probably your daughter!"

Exhausted with the strain of my emotional struggle, still tearful, I knew she was right, but:

"I can't, I just can't."

"You have to, somehow you must, you cannot allow your father to damage one of your children's lives like he damaged yours!"

Those last words somewhere, somehow, in all the mire and darkness found a stronghold, like a tiny wind puff of a seed taking hold and forming a root, and there at the bottom of the pit, the germ was sown, the fragile and hair-thin thread of a lifeline dangling. I had finally reached rock bottom, and there was nowhere to go except up. That lifeline had to be strong enough to hold me until I could start the first hesitant, small steps back up to a new life.

THREE REASONS

Each Day
The hardest thing I have to do
Is to find a reason to survive
To stay alive
To find the strength
To keep on the path
For my allotted span

When the sun shines it is easier
As I look through my window and see
The tiny birds, blue, yellow grey
Clinging precariously with fragile feet
To the nut pens
As to life itself

I can watch the bright green leaves
Flashing and waving in the sunlight
Catching the life giving warmth
At the top of the highest trees
Beckoning to that clear blue world above
And I feel too
The warm breath of life
Filling me with hope

On darker days
The clouds and stormy skies
Reflect my sombre moods
And breaking heart
When all I see
Stretching before me is the lonely struggle
And desolation
Of an empty and loveless life

And I wonder
Why?

Why struggle and fight until the inevitable end
What reason to keep from sleeping, and by that sleep
To finish the eternal fight and find
At last
Peace

I have not one single reason
No – I have three
Three people
Children
Born into life through my very own body

How can I leave them?

To wonder
Why?

What did I do wrong?

Loving them is all I need
Is reason enough to stay alive and live my life
A life that is precious
Because of them

CHAPTER 23

Having been in the clinic for some three weeks, I started to break down barriers with one or two of the other women, and had become quite friendly in particular with two. Whilst details were not discussed we had each acknowledged that the reason for our being in the clinic was childhood sexual abuse, and I think this encouraged a bond between us. The bond remains to this day, and whilst not close friends we still keep in touch.

Lydia, a petite, attractive blonde, was the least communicative of the three of us, but was articulate and intelligent and could always be guaranteed to offer a smart, funny remark if the conversation flagged. Dorothy was dark haired, pale and very self-effacing and had been badly affected by her past experiences. But her very softness and vulnerability made her easy to talk to and confide in. I think that she hid her weakness and fears behind a front of being everybody's friend. Unfortunately for her, this did not help her healing programme, and to my knowledge she was never able to release her anger as I was. She was still visiting the clinic and receiving psychotherapy some two years after I had left, and I know she still finds life a struggle. She latched onto me, we became friends, and though still observing the unwritten rule of not discussing details of our past we were able to intimate a great deal of each other's hurts.

Fresh coffee was always available in the reception area after the morning exercise class, which was then followed by a therapy class run by two of the nurses. I say therapy class, because I have never experienced anything like them, and cannot think how else to describe them. Whilst on the surface they appeared innocuous – in fact we felt rather silly playing at being 'washing machines' (for the uninitiated this means moving around together in a tight group and hugging or touching each other in passing, simulating clothes in a washing machine) – we soon came to learn that these 'games' were designed to bring out deep, buried emotions, and in some cases, especially mine and Dorothy's, cause extreme reactions.

These classes were held in the main lounge, and the only acknowledgment of the fact that we would be moving around was that some of the sofas and chairs were pushed to the sides of the large room. Dorothy and I were unable to hug 'other people', and so we would establish our own private twosome by sitting tightly together, hunched over our morning coffee in close conversation, and when the nurses opened the doors indicating that they were ready and we should come in, Dorothy and I would stick together, like glue. The clinic was mixed, so there would be a male presence in most of the group activities, which in respect to my particular problems caused additional complications. I was, and still am, very clear about my personal space, and do not like strange men moving uninvited into it.

The activities, unless specifically requiring us to be on our feet – e.g. washing machines – were carried out on the floor. Had we been allowed to sit in the armchairs it would have been easy, if we wished, to close ourselves off from the proceedings. Squatting on the floor, uncomfortable and close to the next person, created a sense of vulnerability. Looking back, I can understand that this was all part of the stripping down of our self-imposed imprisonment from the rest of the world, breaking down the barriers that we had each set up to protect ourselves from hurt or unwanted intrusion. A painful but necessary process, for with these barriers intact our inner hurt and anger could not be released. Without this release our depressions and emotional struggles would never cease.

One morning, sitting in our normal raggedy circle, Dorothy and I still next to each other, we were handed a large piece of blank, white paper and a pencil. The nurse asked each of us to draw a large circle on our sheet of paper. She then asked us to think about places and people and 'things' in our lives where, or with whom, we felt safe or unsafe. She asked us to draw pictures inside and outside the circle representing this. 'Safe'= inside the circle, 'unsafe'= outside the circle.

I sat thinking, somewhat confused, because I realised that I could not think of anyone or anything to draw inside the circle. Hesitantly, because I was shocked at my discovery, I drew a few stick men, a house, and I think a boat, outside the circle. Did this represent Fritz's boat? Then I became stuck. I could not think of anything or anyone to put inside the circle. Nothing came to mind – except one thing. Inside the circle I drew a car. I knew for certain, that was the one place where I felt safe. Odd though, because it would only be true if I were driving, which in the recent past I had not done.

Of the others that I could see, there seemed to be a fair mix of objects drawn both inside and outside the circles. I handed in my sheet of paper, apologising,

"I'm sorry but…"

The nurse interrupted me gently,

"No worry, you must express it how you feel it really is."

Once all the papers were handed in, without looking at their contents, she placed them in a folder. I believe we were all wondering what the point of the exercise had been; in my case it had made me feel pitiful.

"We shall do this exercise again in a couple of weeks, and then I shall give these back to you, so that you will be able to see the difference, to measure how far you have come."

And so she did, and my next sheet of paper had my house, and one or two stick people inside the circle as well as my car. So the healing was measurable.

Another one of their 'games' was more far reaching in its effects. Sitting in our usual uneven circle the nurse placed in front of each of us, face down on the floor, two cards – like large playing cards.

"Leave them face down; don't turn them over until I ask you to."

One by one each person was asked to turn their cards over, displaying two words, one on each card, and then asked to express how the two words made them feel. I noticed that normally the two words went together, a matching pair – like 'joke' and 'laugh'. Confident that I could do this I took my turn. Kneeling next to Dorothy I turned my cards over, placing them face side up on the floor, displaying my two words.

LOVE AND SEX

'Love' and 'sex'
Two little words
Seven letters
Seven shaped
Curving
Straight
Lines
On blank white card

So simple
Yet so evocative
So simple
Yet so powerful
Her mind decodes
Those seven symbols
And cries aloud

"No they cannot be
Together
This is wrong"
Something was lost
Surely
In translation

But
The point of reference is skewed
How can her mind ever decipher
These symbols
These words
This meaning
When
In her head
She holds
The wrong dictionary?

Rejecting this pair
This abomination
Her mind revolts

And from the anguish
And despair
So deeply rooted
Within the darkest corners of her memory
A base and primal roar
Tears her throat
Like a jagged blade

And with this scream
Understanding is born
Suddenly
With shocking and painful clarity

Knowledge
That the code she holds
Is warped
Perverted
Useless

And will never open
The book
Nor turn the pages
That reveal the magical story

A birthright
Of every little girl
Listening and waiting
At her father's feet

Charging around the inner circle on all fours, like a child in a tantrum, I grabbed and shoved at all the cards, tearing at them, uncontrollable anger spilling out. The group scattered, shocked. I stood up and ran at the nearest pillar screaming, thudding it with my fists. The nurses quickly cleared the room, leaving the two of them and me, trapped inside. Swept away on this rushing river in full flood, frustrated, unable to find a means to express the full stream of rage, I aimed at anything and everything I could, banging my fists on tables and chairs, stamping my feet and shouting until my throat was raw. Suddenly breaking into midst of my private hell, a firm but calm voice at my side,

"Not the pillar, not the table, you'll hurt yourself, use the pillows, use the cushions, hit them as hard as you can, beat them up, picture him, picture them, let it go, let it out."

And so I did, hitting and punching and crying out my hurt, releasing my repressed anger until eventually, I collapsed, exhausted, into a heap on the floor, quiet sobbing and shivering breaths gradually taking over from the storming rage.

This proved to be the first of many similar outbursts, and I learned that it was OK to let my anger go, in this safe environment. The word would go out: "Jacki's off again" and the room or hallway would clear, and I would be left to release a little more of the filthy stream; formed like an oil deposit over many years, held under pressure, until the thick, black mass was finally tapped and allowed to flow upwards and outwards. Would my source ever run dry?

Woven through these sessions with the nurses were my weekly meetings with John. He continued as ever, in his quiet patient way, allowing me to set the pace and topic. Sometimes frustrated by his refusal to judge or comment on the rights and wrongs of my views, I would get angry with him. Our meetings were in the small library, and I once grabbed a book from the nearest shelf and threw it at him, furious that he would not give his opinion on whether Fritz was right for me or not. He remarked that if he gave me the judgment, it would be just another man telling me what to do. Of course he was right, but I did not want to see that. I was unused to making my own decisions, and judgments. And I suppose that I could not blame myself if the decision proved to be wrong and someone else had made it for me.

CHAPTER 24

A continual stream of people passed through the clinic whilst I was there, staying anything from a few days to a number of weeks. I recall some younger women who came to look upon me as a mother figure, but for others I was a contemporary. One, bird like, very bright and intelligent, blond girl called me 'pretty shoes' because she liked the shoes that I wore. Another began to lean heavily on me as a mother confessor figure, and wouldn't leave my side. Eventually I asked the nurses to talk to her, with the result that she teamed up with another girl, and I became the victim of a whispering campaign of intense dislike. The second girl became particularly vindictive towards me, even within the group sessions. She later confessed that I reminded her of her mother with whom she had a love/hate relationship. Unless they got out of hand, the therapists and nurses tended to ignore these undercurrents of emotions. I guess they are an inevitable part of any closed community, and probably looked upon as a necessary part of our toughening up process.

Everyone dreaded the compulsory afternoon group therapy sessions. Each of us was expected to talk; but not wanting to, we would sit in the circle of chairs waiting for someone to be brave enough to break the silence. Our problems were just that – our problems – and no-one was in a hurry to air them in public. It was a standing joke that we all knew exactly how many tiles there were on the wall above the picture rail in the lounge. I had counted the tiles, the cracks, and devised mathematical formulae for the number of larger squares the tiles formed along the wall by the time I left. There was, however, one good thing that came out of these sessions.

When I had been experiencing the uncontrollable outbursts of anger, one of the nurses had suggested that I write. Anything, whatever I was feeling, just get it out onto paper. In that way, she suggested, I might be able to express my anger in another format rather than feeling so frustrated about it. So I had made some attempts, and my first script consisted of two sides of A4, written in an effort to try and understand why some men hated women. 'An explanation of misogynists', by Jacki G. I showed it to Maurice, who nodded sagely, then grinned at me. My next attempt, however, was the poem that I wrote about Kate's birth. I showed it to the nurse who had suggested I write, and she asked if I would read it to the group that afternoon, as she was running it specifically for women. It took a great deal of courage, but I did read it aloud, and was extremely touched to look around the room when I had finished, and to see some tears but also admiration. Encouraged by their reaction, I continued to use writing as a means of expressing my feelings.

Another suggestion was that I write to my father, to try to express all the rage that I should have been able to let out at the time of the abuse. It was not intended that I post the letter. The simple fact of placing my feelings outside of me, onto a piece of paper, would release some anger and help with my healing. I did write a letter. I have no idea now exactly what I put in it, though I can imagine it would have been a scrambled, furious outpouring of my angst. And I posted it. Not immediately. It sat on my dressing table for some time. I could not put it away. But, eventually it took on a life of its own, becoming the very heart of my rage, taking on a value beyond that of paper and pen and a few scribbled words. Through this letter I felt that I could truly return the hurt to its rightful place.

Some two or three years before, during my early consultations with John, he had enquired if I had brothers or sisters. I told him that I had two brothers, and that they both had daughters. John had told Philip and me that they must be made aware of my abuse because their daughters were at risk. At the time this shocked me. Realization that others could be at risk from my abuser must have helped with my gradual understanding that I was not the guilty party, but it was nevertheless too awful to contemplate that my father could, (or worse maybe already had), abuse his granddaughters. We invited my brothers to come and see us at home, and we told them what had been happening to me and why. From that instant the dynamics of our whole family changed and the far-reaching effects would rattle down the years. What would they do with this terrible knowledge? Their reactions, and those of their wives were all different, and I judged, correctly or not, that there was initially some disbelief. How else could they cope? I do know that one brother continued to allow his daughter to stay, on her own, with my parents. When in later years I tackled him about this, his only comment was that she had been told that she should tell mummy and daddy if anyone ever 'touched her bottom'. His response epitomizes the sad lack of understanding of the way that abusers are able to work and bind their victims to them. And the fact that, in effect, he was prepared to risk it happening, even once, appalled me. Did they say anything to my parents? I was unaware of any reaction at the time.

My letter from the clinic similarly received no immediate response. My parents refused to come out and fight. So I was left holding the baby and the dirty bathwater. In fact the whole stinking mess just sat in my lap. And this, John advised me, was one of the reasons why it was so difficult for me to offload the hurt.

The older women in the clinic, having more in common; not necessarily their problems, but marriage, children, babies, husbands – all easy topics of conversation to slip into, generally sat and chatted together. I did not volunteer friendship easily though, and tended to rely on Dorothy to introduce me to others whom she had already probed and questioned and become close to.

There was one lady in particular whom Dorothy befriended, but whom I tended to steer clear of. Like me she was generally uncommunicative. Unlike me she was rather large, always dressed in baggy tracksuits, shuffling along rather than walking, with her head tilted downwards, giving out an air of great sadness and helplessness. I avoided her because I had a strong conviction that if I offered the hand of friendship she would become like a limpet and cling to me for support. A selfish attitude, perhaps, but at that time I was unwilling to give of myself to anyone. Although, by the time that she came into the clinic I was gaining strength, both physically and emotionally, and growing in confidence. Confidence, that is, defined within the bounds of the very small and safe world in which I currently existed. I was very comfortable and did not want any complications.

The staff had become confident that I would not attempt to kill myself again, and so I was allowed to use the swimming pool without supervision. I would often go in there just to sit on a lounger and read in solitude, to feel the warm spring sun through the windows and lose myself in a book. So, late one afternoon, I walked into the poolroom, fully clothed and intending not to swim but to grab some precious time alone. As I walked around the side of the pool towards my favourite spot by the windows I noticed some clothing floating in the pool. Taking a second look, I realized that it was not clothing, but a person, floating face down in the pool. At the same instant the door opened and a young man, dressed in a towelling robe, came in. I shouted to him, pointing into the pool. Unhesitatingly, he dived into the pool, swam up and under the body and pushed it towards the side where I was waiting. He pushed, and I struggled to pull and lift. She was a dead weight in her sodden tracksuit, far too heavy for me to lift out. Other hands and arms appeared, and between us we managed to pull her out onto the poolside. My feelings overcoming any basic knowledge of life saving, I rolled her onto her side, slapped her face hard and screamed at her in anger:

"You stupid bitch, it's not that bad!"

My anger dissipated instantly, as I remembered someone speaking almost those same words to me two weeks before, words spoken though, in a much more kindly way than I had to this poor lady. I sobbed and cried and held her in my arms, relieved that neither she nor I had succeeded. How tenuous the hold on life can be, how very soon the human spirit can change direction, flick a minute switch and move the track that our life runs along from unbearable to bearable. And just as quickly, back the other way.

She came the following day to thank me, and I was embarrassed. Embarrassed that I had screamed at her in anger when I should have comforted. "I did not do it myself, could not possibly have rescued you without the physical strength of others." But she looked upon me from that day on as her saviour.

I was not so lucky with another patient. She joined us in early March 1995. I shall call her Sandra. Very well educated, well spoken; she had told us one evening when we gathered in the lounge for our usual round of stories, jokes and comments on the day's events, that she travelled a great deal and spoke at all sorts of conventions and meetings. I felt some empathy with her current situation, having experienced a similar change in circumstances. She was totally confused by what was happening to her, unable to understand or accept that she could not be blamed for what she was experiencing. She demanded perfection from herself, and continually chided herself on her inability to function as she felt she should. Her husband visited her most evenings, but it was painfully obvious to me that he was very embarrassed at this unexpected and apparently unwarranted change in his wife.

I was sitting opposite her at dinner one evening, and noticed that her hands were shaking, unable to control her fork. As I watched, a sudden jerk sent a pea flying through the air into someone else's dinner.

"Oh!"

Her cry of shock and mortification caused all eyes to look up. My reaction, natural and easy, was to burst out laughing. She looked over at me in shame, and a poignant memory flashed back of a woman struggling with her own soup-spoon. I went to her, cuddled and comforted, tried to explain that it really did not matter, that I, we all, had experienced the same problem. She accepted my solace gratefully, but I could sense that her distress was not relieved, and she refused to eat another mouthful. Perhaps it was the common factor of us both being businesswomen, or my rush to comfort her, I don't know, but we bonded and became friends, and I took it upon myself to encourage her to tackle the different activities and craft works that were available. We were often to be found late into the night working at a particularly complicated jigsaw puzzle in the art room.

Late one night I was woken by a commotion outside my bedroom. I peeped around the door and saw one of the night duty nurses, a particularly small lady, struggling at the top of the stairs with a man who had been brought in earlier. Knowing that she could not hold out against this powerful man, I ran across the landing intending to help her. As I reached them, the second nurse ran up the staircase, two at a time, with a syringe in her hand. Simultaneously, their training kicked in and both nurses shouted at me:

"Stay back!"

The syringe plunged. Strenuous breathing slowed, and strength ebbed as the drug took effect. Between them they dragged the man away to his room, calling to me to go back to bed. As I stood there, not sure whether to laugh or cry at what I had witnessed, I became aware of another pair of eyes peering round a door at me. It was Sandra. She had heard the commotion but been too frightened to open her door. She looked at me, beseechingly, needing comfort and company.

"Fancy a hot chocolate?"

She nodded her head. I ran downstairs to the kitchen to make us a mug each. We sat together in her double bed, clutching our drinks, mulling over the past hour's events. One of the nurses must have returned to my room to check me, and discovered I was not there. She reminded us of house rules – no going into each other's rooms. We put forward the case that tonight was an exception, that I was trying to comfort Sandra, but I think that they had had more than enough to cope with for one night, and were nervous of being caught letting residents 'break the rules'!

The events of that night cemented our relationship, and Sandra subsequently told me a little of her circumstances. Her family life – an interfering, resident mother-in-law, a weak husband, and her own self imposed demands for perfection had all contributed to her breakdown. She left the clinic before me, not leaving any of us a contact address or telephone number, though we had given her ours, and it was with a combination of anger and great sorrow that I heard, a year later, that she had hanged herself. I cried for several days, furious with her, asking myself:

"Why didn't she call?"

But then, I of all people should have known the answer to that question.

CHAPTER 25

I passed my 47th birthday in the clinic and, as a special treat, Philip and the children were allowed to take me out for Sunday lunch. I have a photograph of us sitting at the table, and I have the impression that I am just that, a paper cut out of myself, something that has no depth or substance. As though I am not really there. My family were all aware of and I think a little shocked at my fragility, and my fear of being outside the clinic. I have a strong memory of them all closing in around me as though to protect me, but also a sense of their embarrassment, almost of a wish to disassociate themselves from this person who was not the familiar wife or mother, but a stranger; frightened, unconfident, unsteady. Their mother had been strong, confident, in full control at home, work and life in general. Where had she gone? They did not ask, and I could not have told them. She was still there, somewhere, having exchanged places with the frightened little girl who was now experiencing the long awaited opportunity to express her anguish and her anger, a little girl who was now often the dominant partner in the dance of the grown woman and child. With time, encouragement and healing, the exchange could turn full circle and the little girl would find her rightful place in memory, and settle quietly, knowing that she was loved and cared for, and that she would never be hurt again.

Because our days were structured and we were expected to attend all the programmes on offer, visiting was kept pretty much in line with normal hospital routine. Occasionally people from the church would visit, but as I have said, Michael kept this to a minimum. Eileen Stearn visited me, and because she could not drive, was accompanied on her visits by her close friend Barbara; white haired, homely and jolly with the giggle of a little girl, an ex-missionary who had worked for twenty-four years in Thailand. Unlike the visits from my children, where I was all too aware of my inadequacy and the subtle shift in my position from mother carer to mother dependent, and the unspoken but assumed expectation that once home I would immediately switch back into that role of strength and competence, their visits were gentle but important reminders to me that there could be a secure life outside the closed world in which I was living. That there were kind and good people who cared about me very much, with no preconceived expectations of my abilities, and who would provide that all-important handhold that I would need as I rebuilt my broken world.

The meetings with Maurice continued, the conversation casual and undemanding. I was still in awe of him, aware that he was always assessing me and that in his hands was the decision regarding my future. One day in late February I had asked him if I would be going home soon. His answer, that it would be a few weeks yet, gave me a great sense of relief. I was worried about coping with life, living alone, outside the clinic. Though pretty much weekly, his visits were not pre-set like John's. I would always receive a message via one of the nurses when Maurice was coming to see me. So I had no excuse to miss him. One afternoon, I knew that he was coming to see me at around 4.30pm, and I left the clinic before he was due. I didn't understand why, but I did not want to see him. I walked and walked for miles, towards the town, with no idea where I was headed. Eventually, exhausted, I turned into the police station and sat on a bench opposite the reception desk. I must have sat there for over an hour. Nobody spoke to me, nobody appeared curious as to why I was there. People came in, carried out their business and left again.

Finally the desk officer asked me:

"Can I help you?"

"No, thank you."

"Who are you here to see?"

"No-one."

He looked at me, obviously perplexed. I started to cry.

"Is there anyone I can call?" he asked.

"My son, please."

Adam was called and came to collect me. I was still weeping and could offer no reason for my escapade. He returned me to the clinic, where I was greeted with some relief, but not annoyance. I was late for dinner, but they found me something to eat and no questions were asked. The next time that I saw Maurice all he said was:

"Well, I was here on time last week."

Was I concerned that he would soon suggest that I went home? Perhaps I could not face this. Perhaps it was easier just to not be there when the time came for difficult decisions. I still had a way to go yet.

It is easy to become institutionalised living in an environment where one is cut off from the normal responsibilities and problems of work and home life with no decisions to make and your day is structured for you. It is an all too simple transition to become accustomed to and content with this greatly simplified version of living. Stepping back into the real world becomes more difficult and frightening with the passage of time, and a stage is reached when it is likely to be impossible to just move back in and pick up the mantle of 'normal' life. A gradual acclimatization must take place.

To this end, the nurses would occasionally take a small group into the nearest town for a short shopping trip. The time came when it was my turn to join this elite group. I was excited at the prospect of getting back to normality, but also somewhat apprehensive. I hung back as the group excitedly left the minibus and set off. I would much prefer to remain in my seat and watch the world from the safe confines of the bus. However, I knew that at some stage I had to take this next step and now was as good a time as any. Walking at the back of our line with my head down, trying to shut out the sounds and sights of strange faces milling and pushing in around me I felt like an oddity, a freak. Each of us within our own shell, the group as a whole also took on a cloak of insularity, and thereby an appearance of something out of the ordinary. I think that day I may have come close to comprehending how physically disabled people must feel when they are subjected to curious public scrutiny.

I had become friendly with a jolly Irishman who had been admitted to the clinic for electric shock therapy. His stoicism in the face of these appalling treatments was admirable, and he became a strong member of our little group. Towards the end of my stay, he and I would be allowed to go to the pub on Friday evenings, a few hundred yards along the road, ostensibly to join the quiz night. Sitting beside him, in the small cosy bar, my mind occupied and challenged with the quiz questions, I felt quite safe. The drugs that we were all taking strictly precluded alcohol, but this did not deter him from his pint of Guinness.

Having coped with the trip into town the next step, as far as the nurses were concerned, was to go out to the small local shops either alone or with a friend. So when one day my Irish friend offered to take me to a small supermarket about a mile away, the staff readily agreed. I think he wanted time to choose a card for a friend, so once we had passed through the entrance doors, we parted, agreeing to meet at the other side of the checkout, and he walked away leaving me standing there alone. Anxiety set in as I looked around the store. I became overwhelmed by its vastness. Memories from childhood encapsulate things as enlarged so that when we return as adults we are surprised by their smallness. I was an adult, but viewing the store through a child's eye.

VISIT TO THE SUPERMARKET

"Stay here
Please
I'm frightened."

The child's voice
Translates its fear into words
No need to be spoken aloud
They are transmitted
To the adult
From the child
Living
Within her

She replies
In words that are unspoken
Yet understood
As thoughts conveyed
Trying to overcome
The child's fear

"Why be afraid?
Come on
You'll be fine
Just move forward slowly,
Down the aisle
Hold the basket."

But
Her legs refuse to move
Rooted to where she stands
Half way along the crowded shopping lane

"I can't
All these people
They're frightening me

They're too close
They're pushing me
I can't breathe
Please
Take me out of here
I want to go home."

She insists
Trying to take control
Of this childish panic

"Look
Just a little further
There's the corner
More space
Fewer people
It'll be better there
Please
Just a little further."

Reaching the corner
She stands
Looks either way
Along never-ending corridors of shelves and produce
And sees
No way out
Busy people
All trapped
Within this heavily populated box

The battle for domination
Lost

The child demands
"I feel sick
I shall be sick
Please
Take me out of here"

The woman struggles for control

"I can't
I'm scared
I'm frightened
I can't breathe
I feel sick
Take me out of here."

Backing into the corner
Needing to know that whatever is behind her
Cannot move
She stands still
Overpowering emotions from the child
Binding and bewildering the two

Eyes downcast
Tears forming
Weeping
A child's voice speaks aloud

"Help me
Please."

"Please
Help me
Please take me home."

Kind voices break through the fearful mist:

"Are you all right dear?"

Unable to speak, looking at them with eyes brimming with tears, I stood there trembling. A member of staff came to our aid, and I was gently taken by the hand and led through the store towards the checkout. My legs refused to work properly and it seemed an age before we completed that journey. My Irish friend was there, waiting, assuming that I was taking longer than anticipated to complete my shopping. He was mortified when he saw me, held between members of staff, softly weeping, unable to explain. He took me by the arm, and seeing a familiar and friendly face I released myself into his care. And we went home.

CHAPTER 26

My weekly meetings with John continued. He took a very passive approach to his work; I often became very frustrated with him, and his attitude would provoke furious outbursts. Perhaps that was his intention, considering the view that he held at the beginning of our relationship when he said that I needed to vent my anger on a man. Our discussions almost always, therefore, centred on my relationships with the various men in my life; my father, Philip, Fritz. John now knew in great detail the story of my abuse; at least that which I had so far been able to recall under his gentle questioning. On behalf of the male species, he had taken everything I could throw at him, verbally and physically. Never before had I been able to express my feelings to a man so forcibly and yet without fear of punishment.

Nevertheless, I sensed that we were coming to another natural end in our talks. I was surprised, therefore, when one day, he asked me what I felt about my mother.

"I love her."

He hummed his response.

"Why do you ask?"

I couldn't understand why but his question worried me. I went on, rushing to explain that ours had been a difficult relationship because my father had always intervened, always prevented us from spending time together, like the Saturday morning shopping.

"She couldn't help it. It's his fault, everything is his fault," I complained.

It was clear from my defensive reaction that I knew that ours had not been a normal mother-daughter relationship, but I had placed the blame for this fully upon my father.

"What about Kate?" he asked.

"What about Kate?" I replied, not understanding his drift.

"Well, do you have a good relationship with Kate?"

"Yes, of course, I love her to bits."

He asked,

"Would you have allowed Philip to have so much control over your relationship with Kate?"

"No, of course." I stopped, looked at him. And suddenly felt sick.

And then, quietly, softly, he dropped his bombshell.

"It's just that it is very unlikely that your mother did not know what was happening."

I couldn't accept this. Not my mother. I told him he was wrong. There was no way she knew. How could I believe this, because believing it would mean accepting that not only had she known about the abuse, but had allowed it to go on for so many years. No, it could not be. She must have loved me more than this, surely? I had tried so hard to please her, had done so many things just for her. But the tiny seed was sown. Arguments raged back and forth in my head. I mentally added up the pluses and minuses of me as a daughter. My looks, as a child, definitely a minus; my achievements, in some respects a plus, but not in others. I recalled the dance of the Indians! The sultry moods that she had complained about were definitely a minus. And lastly, but by no means least; had I done enough for her? Must be a minus.

LETTER TO MUMMY

Dear Mummy

I wonder if you loved me?
I wonder if you knew me?
Did you ever ask yourself why I was such a quiet child?
Did you ever wonder why I was moody?

I tried to make you love me
I tried to be good

I loved you so much

I thought you were beautiful

I wanted to buy you pretty things
Saving my pocket money week by week
Ready for Christmas
Or your birthday

Do you remember the blue, glass bead necklace?
The one I stood looking at in the shop for hours
Wondering if you would like it
Desperate to buy the right one
Proudly carrying it home
Wrapping it lovingly
Giving it to you
Eyes pleading
Please like it Mummy
I so want you to like it Mummy

But you didn't
Like it

You changed it
For another one

Nicer, wooden beads
Prettier blue
To match your dress

Perhaps you would have liked to change me?
For another one
Prettier
Nicer
To match your dreams

Finally, the day came when, towards the end of one of our meetings, Maurice asked if I would like to go home for a weekend. I looked at him, not knowing what to say. "Yes" and "No" were my immediate reactions. He went on;

"You see, we think that you are ready to go home, but we are concerned because we know that you will be alone and have no immediate support system. So how about a trial?"

I agreed, and my visit was planned for the following weekend. I should leave the clinic on Saturday morning and return for dinner on Sunday evening.

Home. I thought about my little cottage. I had only spent a month there before leaving to go to Holland with Fritz; half the time that I had been in the clinic, so it wasn't exactly 'home' in the full meaning of the word. It occurred to me that I had a house, but not a home. The apartment in Spain held only sad memories; there was no going back to Philip and I did not have any relatives who would take me in. So I had no choice but to return to this little house in Sunningdale and make it my home.

Arrangements were made for my car to be brought to the clinic so that I could drive myself. Had Maurice taken a peek at my first circle – the one that showed that I only felt safe in my car? I packed an overnight bag, and after breakfast on Saturday, said my goodbyes and left. It was a bright morning, and I experienced a sense of freedom on the short drive across country that raised my spirits immensely. At least I could still drive. It was a strange weekend; a 'getting to know you' weekend, between me and my new home. I moved from room to room touching things, re-arranging some of the furniture, placing and replacing ornaments, until I had achieved an arrangement that I could call my own, dispelling any remaining memories of Fritz. The garden was fairly large for a village house, bound on three sides by the house, and high brick walls, one of which was supported by beautiful ancient buttresses. The fourth boundary, on the right, adjoined the village pub garden and did not offer as much privacy, being delineated by some rather tatty fencing and shrubs. I resolved

211

to build a brick wall along that side as well so that I could enclose my new little world entirely.

I wouldn't say that it was a joyful weekend, but I managed far better than I had anticipated, experiencing very few panicky moments, and was able to look upon it as a new beginning; one that would take some effort on my part, but which would give me the opportunity to build a real home for Kate and myself.

There is a saying; something about leaving the feast early. I returned to the clinic on Sunday evening a little sad at leaving my new home, but very tired and quite relieved to be cocooned once again in a blanket of dependency.

My programme was now directed towards my eventual return home, to picking up the threads of normal life, along with the responsibility once again, of looking after Kate and myself. In the meantime, I had another exciting weekend to look forward to, as it had been agreed that Kate should stay with me at the clinic for her next exeat. She arrived on Friday evening, very excited at the prospect of a weekend 'in the clinic' with Mummy. Though looking forward very much to having her to myself for two whole days, I was a little apprehensive as to how it would work. She was coming up to fourteen, fast growing into a young lady, and I was acutely aware that during the past two months, I had almost been a child myself. The balance in our relationship had changed, almost levelling out, and I was unsure how to approach it. But I need not have feared. Kate was bubbly and fun; the younger girls took her to heart and the older women were only too keen to 'mother' her. We used the art room, swam in the pool, and watched TV. Our meals were served, and we shared my large double bed, giggling about the stories of life in the clinic that I was able to share. We also had my car, and went out for Sunday lunch together, just the two of us, giving a much-needed boost to my confidence.

I had one more weekend at home, extending it this time to two nights, after which Maurice decided that I was ready to leave. Our final meeting at the clinic was tough. I had grown fond of him. Despite his austere image he was very kindly, and it was yet another 'Goodbye' in my life. He told me that I should continue with the drugs – anti-depressants and sleeping tablets, and that he would contact me to arrange further meetings at his rooms.

He went on to ask me how my work with John was going. I was honest, and admitted that I felt that John and I had reached an impasse. He did not comment particularly on that, but told me that I needed to continue working, but with somebody who was far more specialized. He said that it might take him some time to find the right person, and that I would have to be patient, but promised that he would make arrangements for me to see a new therapist. I had been in therapy on and off for six years and so accepted his decision without too much thought. I wonder why? Perhaps I viewed it as a lifeline, one that could hang there, in the background, to be used when the clinic was no longer a part of my support system. Or had I simply accepted that therapy would continue to be a normal part of my life?

At any rate, I went home, armed with a selection of drugs, a letter for my GP, and a long list of 'do's' and 'don'ts'. The main 'don't' being 'don't get overtired'. Several of the nurses had confirmed that I should call in whenever I was passing to let them know how I was doing, and I did, particularly in the early weeks, when I had no contact with John or Maurice. I would call for morning coffee, and chat to whoever may still be around from my time. Lydia and Dorothy had by now both left for home. It was an important contact for me during these weeks; the only tie connecting me to a recent past, and a safe, strong one at that. But gradually, my contemporaries left, the nurses naturally became interested in new patients and I began to feel less comfortable there. So slowly but inevitably my visits ceased.

Maurice kept his word and telephoned me some time in June to say that he had found a lady for me to see, but she lived and worked in North London. I was happy to make the drive, and so started a new relationship with a different therapist. Where John's work had been to break down and deal with the mess of my past, Gill's was to help me to build for the future. And to an extent, she succeeded. I gained a little confidence, and some degree of self-esteem. I showed her my poems and she encouraged me to continue writing. And, for the first time, I was able to talk openly to another woman about my experiences. While I think of this now, I realize what a major change this was. Rather than talking to another of the gender who had abused, and who was in my mind collectively responsible, I was able to share my feelings with one of my own sex, one who could possibly even come close to a real understanding of what it must have been like, and how and why I felt the way that I now did.

I settled into my new life, making alterations to home and garden, adding a longed-for conservatory and fitting a wood-burning stove in the small lounge; a reminder of the cosy and comforting times I had spent next to the one at the clinic. I discovered that I really enjoyed gardening, and passed hours cleaning and clearing the old brick path that curved the whole length of one side, past the tall fir tree and down to the small seating area in the corner. I remember it as being a balmy period; a feeling of being cocooned in sunny days, and evenings alone, yet not lonely. But especially, more than anything I enjoyed the weekends that Kate came home from school to stay. I was very content, and the sky seemed permanently blue.

CHAPTER 27

I have struggled to write about the months following my exit from the clinic, and I cannot understand why. As I have said my recollection is of balmy, sunny days, weekends with Kate and enjoyable times remodelling the house. We had also bought two gorgeous, honey coloured, guinea pigs, brothers 'Marmaduke' and 'Clarence'. Taking care of them with Kate, or by myself once she returned to school, helped to build my confidence in another area, as I had always been very nervous of animals.

Still taking anti-depressants and sleeping tablets, I suppose I must to some extent have been floating along in that drug induced haze calculated to soften the blows of life, of one's natural and normal but heightened anxiety levels. Perhaps because the life experience itself was dulled by the drug therapy, the memories of that existence are retained within a colourless, shapeless world, where nothing has defined edges or limits, and is therefore difficult to recall with any precision. There were interruptions in this easy flow, but only in the sense that I was away from home, not in the balance of my emotions. Time passed with an overriding sense that it would be ever thus.

Soon after my return home, Kate had asked if she might leave boarding school and move to a school closer to home, as a daygirl. I had no hesitation, never having been happy with my children being away at boarding school, and was excited to think that she would be at home with me more often. I had harboured some resentment at the extent of influence the teachers at boarding school may have had over my daughter, and was quietly pleased that this would give me more opportunity for input during those formidable early teens. Philip didn't take much persuading so we applied to the local girls day school, an ex-grammar school with an excellent reputation. It was extremely academic, and we were not confident that she would be accepted, but I think in the light of all that had happened to her in the recent past, and the glowing report from her boarding school, she gained a place for September 1995.

Kate and I took two holidays in Cyprus that year, one at Easter and one again in August. The Hotel, recommended by Anne as safe and friendly, was situated on a quiet beach east of Limassol. Kate was a sun worshipper like me, and loved reading, and so our days were spent lying by the pool with our heads immersed in books. In the evenings, she especially enjoyed sitting at the bar with me after dinner, sipping a fancy cocktail – non alcoholic, I hasten to add – and chatting to the waiters, who were all too ready to flirt with a pretty fourteen year old. Takis, the head barman, had taken us under his wing, in turns watching and chatting, and by implication protecting us from any unwanted attention. During the first break we had been brave enough to take the overnight ferry to Israel to visit Bethlehem and Jerusalem, which, at Easter time, was packed, vibrant and exciting. The ferry was pretty ancient and creaky, and the lifejackets left a lot to be desired for fit and security, but we laughed our fears away. Oh, and I was offered two camels for Kate when we found ourselves stranded outside the tourist shop that the remainder of the group were browsing around. Eager young Arab boys admiring Kate's long blonde hair, and her youth, pestered us all the way to the door of the coach, which I hammered on loudly, pleading with the driver to allow us back on board ahead of the end of his scheduled break.

Another break, in June, was also enjoyable, but was more testing of my newfound confidence. I had developed a yearning to visit my apartment in Spain. Obviously friends and family discouraged this, being all too aware that Fritz would probably still be around. Eventually it was decided that I should go, but that Adam, Aaron and their friend Mark, should come with me as chaperones. With three handsome young men by my side how could anything go wrong?

Fritz was still living in the port and inevitably he learned that I was back. Though he made no effort to speak to me or contact me he dogged our every move, turning up in the same bars, and the same restaurants, always seating himself in a position not close to but strategically opposite me. He would stare at me unceasingly from his corner, those dark eyes boring straight through me. What devious reasoning prompted to do this instead of tackling me head on I cannot guess, except perhaps that my entourage were so obviously there for my protection. However, it was unnerving, and whilst the boys laughed it off initially, it soon began to irritate Adam intensely. He had never fully dispelled his anger against Fritz, and his youth and hotheadedness overcame my pleas when one night, whilst I was speaking to someone, Fritz pushed the barrier, passed close to Adam at the bar and voiced an opinion that his relationship with me was distinctly abnormal. A scuffle ensued, Aaron and Mark pulled Adam away, and I was helped from the bar, in tears. Unfortunately, the bar owner was a fellow patriot of Fritz so we were asked not to return.

Despite this incident, we did have an enjoyable week, and I returned home confident that any remaining feelings that I held for Fritz were under control, and I would not fall under his spell again.

During that summer one other wave ruffled the calm of my life. Although not a large one at the time, it seemed unrelated to my future, so its implications went unrecognised for what they were. I rode the blip and thought no more. But the seed sown earlier in that year had taken root, was growing, and would not be smothered.

MOTHER

The telephone rings
As I leave the house
Briefly
Before continuing my errands
I stop, and listen
Hearing the haltering message
Recorded
Left on the tape to be heard again
Or erased
And forgotten
Forgotten?
If only painful memories could be so easily wiped out

The sound of your voice tears apart the fragile fabric of the
peace
That has been slowly building around me
Carefully, brick by brick
Smashed, shattered like a pane of glass
In an instant
The work of months

No!
I don't want this contact
Guilt washes through me
As anger erupts
Why now?
What do you want of me?
Fear quivers the pit of my stomach

I cannot take you in again
I cannot bear the heavy load of your guilt
Along with my own
Cannot allow you to smother the new me
Born again, a second chance

But
I need
Need to know
Did you truly forsake me?
Or is it possible
Just possible
That you did not know
That my suffering was merely the result of your ignorance?
But
Even then, your ignorance is your guilt
Not mine

"To mother":
To care for, to protect
To tend, to nurse

Yes
Inescapably
Your ignorance is your guilt
My need to know
To hear the words from your mouth
Battles against the need
To keep myself
Isolated, remote
Disconnected and therefore safe

You did not listen to me when I cried for help
You chose not to see when I lay in his bed
Your bed
Sickened by myself
An unwilling partner
Crying silently
Words unspoken but projected with pleading eyes
"Mummy, please look, please take me away from this"
You were there
You saw
But you did not heed
The beseeching eyes of your child

I cannot call
Cannot risk the terrible hurt that your words may bring
Nor write
What written words
Could tell of the years of guilt and agony
Of split personality
Little girl
Lover
Now a woman, a mother herself
But inside
Remains a hurting little girl

So I return to the same answer
That will protect me now
As it did then
Push it down
Bury it deep
Carry on with my life

I try
But the cry rises
Forcing up through my throat
Into my mouth
Torn from deep within those buried years
Stinking, foul heap of memories

I don't want you in my life!

I stop the car
Hands fisted, banging the wheel
Ignoring the pain
Hands fighting
Flailing in the air, against
A ghost from the past
That will not be exorcised
That chokes me
And haunts me still

Try
Try to break free
Search for something unsoiled and fresh
No drugs, no clinic
I will get through this
I will

Drive home
Unsteady, but determined
Unload the shopping
Clean the fridge
Feed the guinea pigs
Retrieving sanity through normality

Calmer now
Doubts surface
Feeding my guilt
Should I call?
Should I write?
No
Leave it be
Leave it alone
Danger
Do not touch

It will smoulder
It will flare again
At some future time and place

But that is ahead
Beyond today
This is now
Deal with now
Deal with me

Mother
Can wait

The telephone message was accusing. She had seen 'a letter' that I had written to my father.

"Why was I telling these awful lies?"

"Why was I trying to destroy their marriage?"

At last I had a response. Not the happy ever after one that I may have wished for, despite the certain knowledge that this would be impossible:

"We're sorry, please forgive us. We love you."

But the gauntlet was thrown, smacking the ground decisively between us, lying in that no-man's land where, 'til then, no-one had dared to tread. The genie was out of the bottle and could never be recaptured.

Was this what John had been waiting for? He had told me that he believed there was more, much more buried within that he was unable to bring out. I must have told Gill of the call, but I cannot remember her response. Sensing, probably, that it would be the start of another tortuous journey, I felt this was not an issue I wanted to delve into at that time. Or possibly, unable to deal with the terrible knowledge that her mother was still choosing his side, my little girl took control and chose to keep quiet about it, as she had done all those years before? Whatever the reason, I swallowed hard and carried on with my life, not yet ready for another battle that would leave me bloodied and bruised.

PART 4: LEON

CHAPTER 28

Later that year found me back in Cyprus. Alone this time, I had arrived early evening on November 5th 1995. Opening the large sliding doors onto the balcony, I could see a small marina over to my left, and stepping out, I heard a loud whoosh as a shooting flare lit up the sky over the silhouettes of the boats, announcing the beginning of the firework display. I watched for a few moments, and then stepped back into the room. My suitcase lay on the bed, unopened. What should I do now? Unpack, and then what? I decided that there were two options open to me. I could either order room service and watch TV, or take courage and go down to the hotel bar, hoping Takis would be there to chat to. I knew from my last two visits to Cyprus, earlier in the year, that he would probably be in his usual position, at the far end of the large semicircular bar, standing by the till, watching his waiters at their work, checking every transaction. But what if he wasn't? Perhaps tonight was his night off? Alone this time, unsupported by Kate's bubbly presence, and the ease of slipping into a conversation with her and the waiters, I knew if Takis was not there, it would be tough to walk into the bar alone, slip onto a bar stool and order a drink.

A woman sitting in a bar with a young daughter has an air of respectability, but a woman, especially an attractive one, sitting in a bar alone, does not. It is as though a huge question mark sits over her head, begging an answer. And without a thick wrap of confidence around her shoulders, she will worry at this question and supply the answer herself. Single men, standing at the bar will glance across, hoping to catch her eye. And if she looks up, the dance will begin, those awkward but predictable first steps of establishing basic facts upon which the remainder of the evening, and night, will hang. Predictable, insulting and discomforting. Couples sit around in mutual silence, sipping at their drinks, each partner bored, all interesting topics of conversation gone when the children left home, or the daily report from office activities and gossip ceased to be fresh and exciting. She can only offer the latest reductions in supermarket prices, and he knows not to even try to stimulate with stories of the 'hole in one'. The men sneak glances in her direction, their eyes hurriedly dropped, and followed by cold stares from wives, sending out the predictable message: 'Do not touch, private property, don't even think about joining us for company or casual conversation'.

Do I yet have the confidence to hold my head high and take the long walk through the bar and over to a single bar stool, or will I turn heel and take the soft option of TV and an early night?

I watched the end of the display and unpacked my suitcase. Without actually making a conscious decision, I chose and dressed in my favourite "little black dress", picked up a handbag and left the room. A small indecisive step, simply a matter of a determined mind over an unwilling heart, but one that would ultimately prove to be life changing for me.

As I walked through the entrance to the bar I could see Takis at the till. A flood of relief ran through me. He looked up, smiled and nodded towards a stool next to his favourite spot. By the time I reached it, there was a gin and tonic waiting for me. I could have hugged him. He explained that he knew I was coming – as head barman he was always given a list of new arrivals. The evening passed quickly, as we chatted and he worked. Beyond midnight the bar began to empty, but I noticed that a man who had been sitting alone further along the bar from me, was still there. Takis was speaking to him and I guessed they must be acquainted. He was dark complexioned with black wavy hair, tall and physically well built. In fact, quite a dish. As Takis walked back behind the bar towards me, the man left his stool, but instead of heading out of the bar, he came towards me, smiling. Takis introduced us: his name was Leandros. They were old friends, used to work together, but he was now living in England. He was staying at the hotel next door for a two-week holiday. His English was impeccable, and the three of us talked, laughed

226

and joked for the last half hour whilst Takis closed down the bar. Finally, I said goodnight, and left them to go to my room. I fell asleep thinking of the tall, dark handsome stranger!

The next morning, I was awoken by the telephone on the bedside table. I looked at my watch, 8.30am. Who could possibly be calling me? A flash of panic, Kate, but no, I had not left a contact number, and yet Anne would have known how to reach me. I picked up the handset. "Hello?"

I recognised the voice, which spoke without preamble or giving me space to interject – "Good Morning, it's Leon. It is raining today, and you cannot sunbathe, so I would like to show you my island."

"Er, yes fine, lovely, thank you. But what time?"

"I am downstairs in the lobby, I'll wait for you."

I negotiated a half hour in which I could shower, dress and collect my wits.

He was right, the weather was not conducive to sunbathing, and it drizzled on and off all day. True to his promise, he showed me a great deal of the island. His passion for Cyprus, his intimate knowledge of the island and his bubbling personality were infectious, and I enjoyed the day immensely. That evening he took me to dine in a steak house, run by another old friend in Limassol. He encouraged me to drink red Cypriot wine, and eat olives. As he left me, much later, he asked where I might be the next day if the sun was shining. By the pool of course! Close to the pool bar!

The following morning, glorious sunshine filled my room so I was up early and down to the poolside. I was sitting at the bar sharing a coffee with another resident, a man who I suspected was trying to sell me a line, when looking over his shoulder I saw Leon walk through the gate in the hedge between our two hotels. Dressed in his swimming costume and carrying a plastic bag of beach essentials, he had a huge grin on his face and was looking very pleased with life until he saw me, sitting at the bar with a man. His smile disappeared, and he started to turn away, looking embarrassed. Somehow, I immediately sensed that he was not angry but disappointed. I also knew that he would not force his attentions on me, unlike the man who had bought me coffee. With a quick apology I slipped from the bar stool, and called out: "Leon, hi!"

And that was all it took. We spent the remainder of my week together, each day sunbathing, swimming, touring if the weather was poor, and every night we dined in the most wonderful Cypriot restaurants, by the sea, in the mountains, in the pretty villages, all tucked away from the busy tourist routes.

I can hear you thinking, "Here she goes again". But this time I was wiser, and Leon was not Fritz. He was open, relaxed, warm and friendly. And I didn't fall into the relationship so devastatingly suddenly. It was a slow realisation that maybe, just maybe, here was a man I could simply have fun with. No demands, no strings, complications, or expectations. Just seven days in which we could enjoy each other's company. When the day came for me to fly home, he had already cancelled my taxi and decided that he would take me to the airport himself. He suggested an earlier departure from the hotel so that we could lunch at one of our now favourite restaurants on the beach at Zigi before completing the journey to the airport. What I thought would be our last meal together was spent sitting at a table on the water's edge, the afternoon sun glinting off the waves, eating grilled fish and drinking white wine: 'Aphrodite'. A perfect end to my holiday. My description of the holiday to some of my friends has earned me the nickname 'Shirley Valentine', but I didn't elect to stay; I came home. Our goodbye at the airport was warm, though tinged with sadness. But I was determined not to give him any means of contacting me. I liked him, and I was sure that he wanted us to remain in contact, but I was afraid of making any commitment. Away from home the holiday atmosphere was totally separate from real life – it would be unrealistic to think that this was how it would always be. More important, I needed time away from him to think, back in my own world. As I reluctantly moved away into the departure hall, he pressed a card into my hand. I looked at it briefly, it said: 'Leandros Rodikis, Proprietor, and Hotel' – it was his hotel's address and contact telephone number. My eyes returned to his smiling face; big brown eyes staring into mine, hoping for a response?

"Just in case you ever decide to visit Blackpool," was all he said.

Kate was still at boarding school, her weekends shared between Philip and I. My workload with the business, never a demanding nine to five job, was fairly light. So I did have time to think. Something in me wanted to hold back, to stay clear of men – probably the sensible adult part of me. But there was also that little 'What's the harm, why not have some fun?' My social life was non-existent; my girl friends were all married, so it was not easy to get out to meet people. I asked myself how much I liked him, analysed my feelings for him. But then why was I worrying about all this? Why not just take some time out to have fun with a good friend? So eventually, a little unsure of what the response would be now that he too was back at home amongst friends and family, I wrote a short letter, thanking him for making my holiday such a wonderful experience, and for introducing me to his beautiful homeland. At the top of the letter, I put my address and telephone number. I had my answer very quickly. Four days later he called and invited me to Blackpool for a few days. I enjoyed being with him again, and we had a busy few days visiting places in Lancashire that I had not seen, but I was glad to return home to Sunningdale. I cannot explain why – I don't think it was him, perhaps more the 'where' than the 'who'?

It was about this time that Maurice had told me I was probably ready to come off the antidepressants. I was instructed to cut the dose down gradually over a few weeks until I could stop completely. I had no reason for concern. I disliked taking them, and welcomed it as the approaching end to being 'unwell'.

In December I was in Spain again as Adam was using my apartment as a jumping off base for an adventurous trip overland to South Africa by Land Rover, which he and a school friend Nick had been planning since they were eighteen. Though Fritz still chose to hover in the background, we were able to ignore him and there were no nasty incidences. However, Adam fell down two flights of the lift shaft and though he was extremely lucky to escape with a few bruises and a badly sprained ankle, it delayed his departure to Africa by two weeks. I flew home, amidst tearful goodbyes, wondering how his exciting but dangerous trip would pan out, and when I should next see him.

Christmas that year turned into a sad and sorry affair. Leon had wanted me to return to Blackpool and spend Christmas with him, but I declined because Kate and I were going skiing in Canada the day after Boxing Day. Kate and Aaron were committed to have Christmas lunch with their father, but had promised to come round to me later in the afternoon. Philip had taken them to lunch with a friend who was notorious for her lack of timekeeping, and they had not eaten until 5.00pm. They had called me, apologising, but were obviously in the difficult position of being obliged to stay at this friend's house, whilst realising that this meant that I was spending Christmas Day alone. My anger was directed at Philip, as I saw this as being typically thoughtless of him, but my alter ego niggled me, telling me that they were happier with their dad, and were putting off coming to see me. Eventually they arrived at my house mid-evening, both acutely aware of my disappointment. Unable to hide my tears when they arrived I inadvertently added to their guilt and the evening was far from being the relaxed and enjoyable time it should have been. I was so miserable and felt very unloved and unwanted. If a negative inference can be taken from a situation, then I will do so. A remark, a look or an action may not be intended as a rejection but will be taken as such by me, especially if made by someone I care about. Perceived rejection is an extremely destructive emotion for me, and has caused me many painful experiences. It is an emotion governed by the lack of self worth of abuse survivors and needs much hard work to overcome. On several occasions it has even pushed me into a period of deep depression.

Having experienced Christmas alone for the first time I vowed that I would never allow myself to be in this situation again. If I were asked to name the worst aspect of divorce it would be an easy choice – Christmas. Practical difficulties of divorce are soon overcome or accepted as a part of life. Emotional difficulties; sharing the precious times that are spent with children and ultimately grandchildren – birthdays, holidays, school plays – are never truly overcome. But nothing tears at the emotions like Christmas Day. It is painful for all involved. It starts early in the season when tentative phone calls are made to see who is going where and with whom. Some, the strong ones, stake their claim early on and will not be moved. Others will try and please everyone – an impossible feat. Few, very few, are happy just to fall in with the majority decision. A day that should be full of peace and joy, a celebration of our Saviour's birth, turns into an agonising guilt trip, and I have learned over the years that even the best planning fails to mitigate the heartbreak of separated families.

Nevertheless, Kate and I had a wonderful holiday, skiing together in the Canadian Rockies, and the New Year began on a relatively high note.

CHAPTER 29

In January 1996, Leon came to spend a few days at the Old Forge. He was not confident driving on the English motorways and so he travelled down by train. At the last minute the train was diverted so after a desperate phone call I had to drive in to collect him from Paddington in London.

Our first time together at the Old Forge was not a great success. No longer subdued by drugs my anxieties and frustrations were beginning to resurface. I had never been a calm and relaxed person to be around, and perhaps inviting someone into my own personal environment at this time was a mistake. Leon's natural relaxed attitude did not fit into my rigid domestic life order. His physical presence was large, and the cottage small. Perhaps memories of Fritz's control in this area of my life made me wary of what I perceived as Leon's interference. And underneath all this something else was bubbling away. A whole new frontline had been opened up in my war – the likelihood that my mother had colluded in the abuse. Unresolved and repressed feelings centred on her, along with a need to know the truth. The accusing telephone call still remained unanswered. Whether it was instrumental in bringing these issues to a head or not I have no idea, but by the end of Leon's visit I was struggling to keep my head above water. I recall fighting back tears as I drove him to the station. At one point, unable to control my emotions any longer, I pulled over, stopped the car and thumped the steering wheel with my fists, sobbing, and shouting incoherently. He spoke softly, urging me not to cry, but neither asking any questions, nor telling me to pull myself together. I waved goodbye at the station, wondering if he would ever call me again.

DARKNESS

Once again the darkness descends
Like the gloom of an early winter evening
Surrounding and smothering my conscious thought
Numbing all feelings of joy
And bursting the bubbles of my natural exuberance
Leaving me suspended

Floating in a vacuum of indecision
Heavy limbs matching the sodden spirit
Unable to complete even the simplest of daily tasks
The voice of anger inside my head
Demanding release
But remaining
Unexpressed
Suppressed
For the sake of those around me

I search in vain for the inner strength that lies
Buried deep within my very being
The force that has somehow always cut through
The thick, dark fabric of my pain
And released me from this choking of my life's flow

But – for the moment it is elusive
Darting teasingly into the suffocating blackness
Like a wraith
There one minute and then gone
As if 'twere never there

I cannot chase it
My mind struggles with the mundane
To keep the body physical
Functioning
Leaving no room, for flights of hopeless fancy
Which may crash in the fog of despair

Each day dawns
New and promising
To the world outside my window
And I wonder if I will survive
The demands put upon me through the span of another day
By this uncompromising, uncaring world.

By the middle of February I was back in the clinic. Kate, no doubt frightened by the tears and helplessness, had called John. We had just returned home from a trip to the supermarket. She tells me now that John pretty much left her to make the decision, and she had made it, knowing not only that I would be safe in the clinic, but also that she was unable to cope with this situation alone.

The room I was allocated this time was not as large and airy; neither did it have the same outstanding view across the front lawns and garden beyond. It was smaller, darker and I remember being afraid of a large wing chair that was sitting in one corner. So much so that they had to remove it, promising that if a larger room came available they would move me.

This time I refused point blank to go onto anti-depressants. I knew that was not the answer to my problems. The frustrations resulting from the telephone call must have surfaced, as the nurses asked me if I felt able to face my father, to try and place the ball firmly back into his court. Could I visit him, maybe with someone alongside to support me? I knew that was out of the question. I was afraid of him, or maybe it was my little girl who was still afraid of him. Even now, I feel sick remembering how I felt at this suggestion. It was as though by going back into that house, I would be rolling back the years and placing myself back under his control. Rationally I knew that there was no risk. I could run, walk out, and even hit him if necessary. But there is no rationality in deeply embedded fear. It is as though we were, still are, like conjoined twins, not with a physical join, but an emotional one. Despite the years of abuse, he was my father, and a strong, natural bond had existed between us since before my birth, one that would remain until one of us died. For me that link was interwoven with shame, hurt, fear and subjugation, and only by creating geographical distance between us could I keep these feelings under control. It was a vicious circle. Until I could place the guilt where it belonged I would not break the bond. These negative feelings kept me in thrall, and it was some time yet before I would learn that only positive feelings would sever the ties that bound me to him.

They suggested a telephone call – less confrontational - and I agreed that I should. But on a deeper level, my instinct was to run away and forget, not to turn and face and fight. From somewhere, therefore I had to summon the courage for a battle that I was not even sure I should be waging.

I sat on the edge of the bed, rocking backward and forward, indecision tormenting me. Fear fighting a fierce battle with the conviction that this must be done, somehow. I picked up the telephone handset, sat listening to the familiar burr of the dial tone. I pressed the keys, number still easily retained in my memory. Far away, a telephone rang in an unknown room, in a house full of childhood memories. He answered.

CUTTING

It hurt
The cutting
The digging and scratching
It stung

But not enough
Not so as to be unbearable

Tears pouring from aching eyes
Dropped and mingled with blood

Nose streaming
Runnels of mucous
Entering the fray
The mix of tears and blood

The battleground this time
A slim and vulnerable left wrist
Raw skin
Torn away by the determined digging and scratching
Of the blunt tweezers

Somewhere in her brain
A remembered phrase
Better to cut down the vein
Not across
The traditional method

The monster of pain and anger
Turned in on itself
To hurt, maim and punish
Destructive forces turned against the victim

Not the perpetrator
He is out of reach

Out of harm's way
Rebutting
Refusing
To accept the guilt

Rejected
It bounces back
Sucked in
Welcomed back
Come home to mummy
I will take care of you
I will soothe you

Comfortable
At home
It eats, and eats
Destroying its host

Keep going
Keep digging
Scratching and cutting
At the now raw and bleeding wrist

It hurts too much

Coward!

Keep going
Keep digging
Scratching and cutting

Tears, blood and mucous
A sad, crumpled heap
Sobbing, retching
In the corner of a cold dark bathroom
Lodged between the bath and the toilet seat
In an unknown room
Head full of childhood memories

Someone came to my room, later. Perhaps I was late for afternoon tea. I don't know. They were angry with me. Picked me up, cleaned my wounds and put me to bed. I tried to explain. I called him, like you said I should.

"Who? Called who?"

"My father."

Realisation dawning on what I had done, and probably with a better understanding of what had occurred than I had, they comforted me, and gently explained that I should have had one of them sit with me when I made the call. They had not intended that I do it alone, unplanned, and unprepared. Later, much later I told them what had been said.

Without preamble I had accused him, called him a bastard, told him I hated him for what he had done to me. His response was not anger, nor even a raised voice, but he spoke calmly, confidently, once again controlling his prey.

"You are crazy, mad and always have been."

Hearing the familiar, smooth, sneering tone of his voice, I pictured the triumphant smirk on his face, and my resolve was crushed. He knew he had won before we started. My mother's voice broke through the torrent of emotions that were ripping my head apart, shouting at me:

"Will you stop this! Will you stop telling these lies! Why are you trying to destroy our marriage?"

And that was it, my first and last attempt at getting them to admit their culpability.

I stayed another two weeks in the clinic, recovering from my wounds: physically and emotionally. My wrist was very sore, it had been infected, and I was told I would always carry the scars. So what, it could join all the others. I celebrated another birthday. My spirits were lifted to receive a card from Leon. I called him, and explained where I was. "When you get out, you must come up and stay and I will spoil you," was his simple response. Natural and automatic for him, but he had thrown me a lifeline. It was just what I needed to hear. I pondered his words, speaking them aloud, tasting the feel of them in my mouth, in my head. "I will spoil you". Had anyone ever said that to me before? I don't think so. My grandparents had spoiled me, in the way that grandparents do. Philip had cared for me, to the limits of his ability. But never had anyone intimated a wish to spoil me. The enormity of these words, falling onto the ears of one who had always felt unlovable, undeserving, unworthy of any special attention, is indescribable. Looking back now, I can see that these words were the first instalment of the great gift that Leon would ultimately give me.

CHAPTER 30

Nurture or Nature? Which has the stronger influence in the development of child into adult? Mother Nature has been kind to me. She gave me intelligence, a reasonably well-proportioned body, and passable good looks, which were not apparent in childhood, but which I now have the confidence to acknowledge. Nurture must work on what it is given; the raw material to be shaped and encouraged into the end product. Nurture in its kindest mode will enhance inherent characteristics, but if brutal, uncaring or selfish it can also obliterate them, destroying those early shoots that are then never remembered, and must be learned over again. Does God really choose our parents? If so, then there are times when I would accuse him of having a sick sense of humour. But if I reflect on my life I can trace a thread of strength, sometimes lost along the muddy pathways that mapped out my development, but always regaining its foothold. An extra gift, given to a child who would need it to survive the environment she had been placed in. There was an ever-present driving force that would not allow her to give up. Developing from that strength and determination in the face of trial and humiliation was a capability to cope. I left childhood with an entrenched understanding that I had to fight alone, against all odds, if I wanted to survive. This automatic response in adversity – to fight alone – was both a positive and a negative trait. Negative, because it evolves into a tendency to shut out people who are willing and waiting to help. My need to control, although providing some protection against violation, was another by-product of this survival instinct. After all, if I held the reins, I could prevent anything from going wrong. Logical, perhaps, but making no allowance for life's unexpected twists and turns.

And what had been achieved over those seven or eight years, in and out of counselling, eleven weeks in the clinic, and on drugs? Had these further strengthened or detracted from my character?

I had learned that I was not alone, that there were many more women, many more, suffering from varying degrees of emotional damage caused by childhood sexual abuse.

I had learned that my guilt could not be placed where it belonged. Though my father's guilt was clear cut, my mother's was not. Having a daughter of my own, it was beyond comprehension to me that any mother could allow this to happen, year after year to her daughter. And it was this disbelief that kept alive the seeds of doubt; increasing my own guilt, in that I could not love her in the way a daughter should. Though I could feel angry with her for not protecting me, I could still feel guilty at not sending her a birthday card.

I had also released a great deal of anger, in a safe environment. But that was the root of another problem. My anger had been released in rushing torrents, screaming at John or whoever was on duty that day. Released against people who were being paid to listen and to accept whatever I threw at them. Nurture had not taught me that it was permissible to express anger at a loved one, that love would not be lost, and I had still not learned this. The guilt I felt at divorcing their father, breaking up the family, added even more to this fear in relation to my children. The boys were grown men now and had left home, and so the incidences when I may be angry with them were few, but not Kate. She still lived with me and my inability to control and correctly express displeasure would ultimately have a devastating effect on our relationship.

My therapeutic path then, had allowed release and some understanding, but not given tools for recovery, for growth and regeneration. My strength and determination would hold me together until a confrontation arose that threw my emotions into such turmoil that they would not prevail. Patched up, back on unsteady feet I returned home and picked up the reins of my life, little more prepared than before.

I did take up Leon's offer, and our relationship continued intermittently, through the spring and summer. Occasionally I would stay with him in Blackpool. Whenever possible, we would meet in Cyprus, he flying from Manchester a day before me, and me following from Heathrow. It was there, in Cyprus, that I was truly happy with him. I am sure it was pure escapism. Though I was enjoying my new home, Kate was busy becoming a young woman and we were experiencing the inevitable differences in opinion over her life choices. I was often lonely, hungering for adult company, so the times spent with Leon were an exciting and enjoyable break. I knew I was not in love with him. I don't think, at that time, I was capable of loving another man.

I confess I did not like Blackpool. I was a southern girl, no question, and could not find anything there appealing in any way. Leon was there because his ex-wife had wanted to return there when the Turks invaded northern Cyprus. Leon had been managing a five star hotel in Famagusta at the time of the invasion, and he and his English born wife were on a business trip to the UK. He lost everything: house, cars, property; his parents were posted as missing, believed dead, and his children trapped in Cyprus. They were subsequently smuggled out with a group of musicians and brought to England.

In July, Leon announced that he was trying to buy another, larger hotel. I was pleased for him, but I knew this meant that he would be even more tied up in Blackpool, and it forced me to stop and think about whether or not I should continue with this long-distance relationship at the expense of developing a life of my own in Sunningdale.

Kate and I flew out to Spain alone, in August, because Leon was busy with the new hotel. We settled very easily and quickly into our old routine of lazing by the pool during the day, and dressing up each evening to go out for dinner. Kate had discovered that a girlfriend at school would be there at the same time, as her parents had an apartment in the port, so quite often after dinner she would disappear with her friend and some other English youngsters. Despite occasional disputes over her curfew times, and my steadfastness in refusing to hire a golf buggy for her to ride down to the port to meet her friends during the day, we got on well and enjoyed our times together. There is however, one incident, that is worth recording, and which we both look back and laugh about now, but at the time was terrifying.

Long after Kate and I had gone to bed one night, a loud hammering and banging on the back patio door awakened me. A voice was shouting:

"Come out you bitch! – I know you're there!"

It was Fritz. I knew that he would wake Kate but to reach her room I had to cross the lounge, which could be seen through the back patio windows and large open hatchway. I crawled from my bedroom, scrambling across the lounge on hands and knees, keeping my head low. The banging and shouting continued. When I reached Kate's room she was awake, sitting in her bed. Not knowing what to do, or who to call, we simply sat there, clinging to each other until eventually the noises abated, and it fell quiet. We waited a while longer, no further sounds were made, and as she was still nervous I took her back to my bedroom. Within minutes the phone beside the bed started to ring. I knew it would be him, so I left it. Relentlessly it rang and rang. Quietly I lifted the handset off the hook and listened: "Jacki, I want to talk to you!" his voice ranted. I laid the receiver back down, unplugged the telephone, and walked through to the lounge, unplugging the telephone in there as well.

The following morning I called the attorney who had helped us to purchase the apartment and he took me to the Policia to apply for an injunction against Fritz, to bar him from any contact with me, or from coming near the apartment. The final chapter in my relationship with him.

Having closed this door finally, I returned home to England where I closed another. I wrote a letter to Leon telling him that, though I was very fond of him, and it saddened me to break our relationship, I felt very strongly that I must try to focus on building a life in Sunningdale, around Kate, and my own friends. He was a lovely man, and I wished him every happiness, and success with his new venture. His reply was typical, expressing sorrow, and thanking me for the wonderful times we had shared. He told me it had been an absolute pleasure knowing me. No anger, nor recriminations, just respect, both for my decision, and for himself in that he would not plead for a change of heart.

CHAPTER 31

Life in Sunningdale settled into a comfortable routine. I did not make any effort at joining new clubs or making new friends, finding my few, existing relationships sufficient for my needs. I would occasionally call into the village pub next door to my house and more often than not there would be someone to chat to. One of the regulars took me out to dinner once or twice, but he was just as happy as I was to leave it at that, remaining friends who could buy each other a drink and spend time together at the bar.

I attended church most Sundays, finding companionship and friendship. I became involved in coffee rotas, and some fund raising for the Children's Society. My search for something momentous was not successful. The liturgy, the hymns and the token offering of 'the peace' were all without depth or meaning for me. I wanted more, believed that there must be more, could not accept that 2000 years of history and tradition could amount to just this. People had died for this man, had sacrificed their whole lives for him. Why? What had they gained? I looked at the people around me in church, and could not see anything in their make-up that would lead me to believe they had found something special. For me, faith had to be certain, a conviction deep in my heart – it had to be all or nothing, and I was as yet, much closer to the 'nothing' end of the scale.

In November I took a trip to Beijing, where Anne and Campbell were now living, having taken up the offer of his company of a three year re-location. I decided to spend a week in Hong Kong en route. Terrified when the day to leave arrived, Kate and Aaron had to pour me into the taxi to Heathrow airport. Alone in Hong Kong, I forced myself to tour everywhere from Victoria Peak to the busy river, and the crowded, vibrant street markets of Kowloon and thoroughly enjoyed the new sights, smells and sounds that assaulted my senses at every turn. I had a wonderful holiday and returned home with more self-confidence than I had had in a long time.

The depth and darkness of winter has always been difficult for me. My mood downshifts steadily and slowly in pattern with the declining days. Rain pours into my soul as well as onto the ground outside, dampening my spirits and dowsing any glowing fires of joy that may be smouldering inside to keep the heart warm until the spring sunshine can once again encourage new life. By February I was sinking fast into that dark place where hope cannot exist, and the weeping began again.

Kate was packing up her belongings to return to Philip for her two-week stint with him, when the floodgates burst. She found me standing in my bathroom, left arm over the basin, fresh blood running from my wrist. I looked at her guiltily, and we both started crying. I knew, through all my misery that this was wrong, that she should not have to deal with this. But I could not summon the emotional strength required to overcome the destructive forces that were working within me. Tears pouring, I told her I was sorry, promised I would not do it again. Breaking a promise to myself, making a promise to my child that I could not guarantee to keep. She was fifteen, struggling with her own burgeoning teenage emotions and the demands of school exams. How monstrous that she should have to carry this extra burden.

This time it was my GP, a caring young man who came in from his busy surgery, took one look and advised that he was not prepared to leave me at home in this state. I imagine he must also have been extremely concerned for Kate's welfare. I agreed, reluctantly, to return to the clinic. But I refused drugs, and would only stay for a few days, a stay which, once again encompassed my birthday.

Back home very quickly, I muddled on. Emotionally unstable, I was walking a tightrope; the balancing pole controlled not by my own hands and arms, but by outside influences – my interactions with other people. In the main, this was Kate. I have no idea how she felt, nor how she coped with a mother who was persistently so unwell. I was in my own living hell, and no doubt she was in hers.

Kate was still sharing her time between Philip and me. It was only a fifteen-minute walk from house to house, but logistically a complicated transition, packing her ever-increasing parcel of belongings every two weeks, including the guinea pigs! However, her old home must have been a welcome breath of fresh air for Kate. Philip had a new, full life of his own now, and she was allowed pretty much free rein when with him. His life needs had always come first, and he saw no reason to change when Kate was with him. He saw his responsibility as ending with school runs and food shopping. If she were out late on a Saturday night, he would leave her to get a late train home alone, a total dereliction of his parental responsibilities as far as I was concerned, as well as causing me considerable anxiety on an issue over which I had no control. Rightly or wrongly I was far more rigid in my interpretation of the rules, and I resented the time he had with her, feeling that he was the 'goodie' and I the 'baddie'. I believed he was indulging her, spoiling her, even risking her safety. In fact, unwittingly, he was probably giving her the space she needed away from the worry of my yo-yoing emotions. But, I was unable to step outside of my feelings and understand the dynamics of the situation. All I did was to try and control her, believing that my efforts alone would keep her on track with schoolwork, social responsibility and development.

Life throws huge spanners in the works sometimes, and there is no dodging them. It's almost as though there is a giant celestial hand guiding the direction of the fan when the shit takes off. It so happened that Mothers' Day weekend fell during the two-week period that Kate was spending with Philip. I had not discussed it with her when she left to stay with Philip as I had blithely assumed that she would come and spend the day with me. A phone call from Kate on the Sunday morning, saying that she would like to come round and see me left me surprised at the implied brief visit, and I asked if she were staying for lunch.

"No, Dad's getting lunch for me."

All I could think was that my daughter was rejecting me in favour of her father, on Mothers' Day. My feelings of worthlessness overshadowed all sense of perspective, of others' needs, and rationality spiralled away in the tornado of my hurt. By the time she arrived I had worked myself up into a state of extreme agitation.

She was barely into the lounge when I challenged her, angrily. She stood her ground saying that it was her time with Dad, but she wanted to visit me, as it was Mothers' Day. Hurt boiled over into uncontrolled anger, released without thought of the consequences. I shouted that love was not there to be picked up and put down when it suited – if she did not care enough to spend the day with me, she had better go. She stood there trembling, looking at me.

"I bought you this."

She placed a small, flat, square package on the chair, with an envelope. I cannot believe that nowhere within me existed a tiny flicker of sense, desperate to stop this tirade before irretrievable harm was done. But it didn't stand a chance against the maelstrom that had been unleashed. I grabbed her by the shoulders, turned her around and showed her the door. I watched through the window as she walked up the small front path and along the roadway, her head held high, her small, stubborn little chin tilted proudly upward in strength and defiance. Had I any clarity of thought at that moment I would have seen that she truly was my daughter.

I shall never forget that unending minute of time as I watched her walk away. All rage collapsed, to be replaced by sickening despair: What had I done? Cruelly rejecting my daughter's love. I wanted to run after her, cry out and beg her to come back, but I couldn't. My stupid, stubborn determination not to show weakness would not allow me to. So I let her go, slip away from me, a hurt and bewildered little girl.

Why did anger spill over more readily towards Kate than the boys? I was just as much in fear of losing her love as I was theirs. Perhaps the normal teenage daughter/mother angst was being exacerbated by an unacknowledged deep-rooted, envy of her relationship with my husband, her father. Other than being briefly suggested once by John, this issue had never been addressed during counselling. She had received, and was still receiving something that I would never have – the perfect adoration of a doting father and she was receiving it from a man who had also denied me the love that I wanted and needed from a husband. She was the common denominator in this swirl of emotion, a focus for my outbursts, a reason both selfish and childish. Trapped inside me was a frightened child who still waited for the love and attention that was her right.

I cried all afternoon, both angry and distraught that things had gone so badly wrong. Philip called to try and explain, but my anger refocused at him, and nothing he could say made me feel better. Early in the evening the telephone rang again. This time it was Kate.

"Hello Mummy," she spoke tentatively.

"Hi darling, how are you?"

I cannot remember the conversation clearly, only an uneasy sense of where it was heading, and that neither of us could find a way to say the words. I helped her, dreading the answer that I knew was coming:

"What are you trying to say?"

"I want to stay with Daddy."

MAMA I LOVE YOU

"Mama I love you"
Spice Girl's song
CD lovingly chosen
Wrapped with care, and
Given to her mother
By a little girl

A special gift
An expression of precious love
Received not as it should have been
Not graciously
Not with returned love
A hug and a kiss

But rejected in anger
Left unopened while
Angry words were shouted
At a treasured, loved child

The rage spent
On the wrong person
At the wrong time
Pushing away the one gift
That is to be held above all others

Watch her walk away
The picture ever etched into memory
Of a little girl, proud
And hurt

Mother and daughter alike
Must share in the desolation
Of rejected love

But she cannot conceive of
Her daughter's pain

That is lost
In selfish condemnation
Of the child's actions

Her days are lost
In an ocean of pain
So deep
So wide
Rolling dark grey waves
Stretch away forever
To the horizons of her life

A water world
In which she floats
Hot tears flood over aching eyelids
Even as they open
From a dreamless sleep
Before awareness takes over
And conscious thought remembers
Why they are there

Bitter tasting regret
Cannot heal
Nor even soothe
The aching heart
Only provoke
Feed and inflame
The agony of self-loathing

Time cannot be returned
No fervent wishes
No power on earth
Can shift the moment
Back to before

Time cannot undo
Those dreadful deeds
Or unsay those terrible words

But slowly
Surely
Time will begin to heal

We have spoken often of this day, and both have different recollections. I think, in fact I know, that we now have a better understanding of each other's perspective. A grown woman, she is justifiably angry that the decision was not taken out of her hands, that she had to take the momentous step to tell me that she did not want to live with me.

I vividly recall Philip's desperate attempts at retrieving our marriage when I first left him. His offers far too late, to learn bridge, to join my gym, to come swimming with me after work. He was desperately trying to make all the wrongs right, to turn the clock back and have another chance. And now I had some idea how he must have felt. Like clinging on for dear life to the edge of a cliff, knowing with each slip of your straining fingers, that it is already too late. That no matter what you do, however hard you try to hold on, you are going to fall. Now it had happened to me. The matter had been taken out of my control, and I believed that my actions had caused my daughter's love to slip away. Whereas the reality was that she did love me, very much, but self protection had lead her to make a very hard decision.

I cannot express the desolation that was my home for the following days and weeks. I cried. I sobbed. I punished myself with recriminations. That night I had called Mary, who offered to drive down from Cirencester and stay with me. But I could not allow her to. She had her own family commitments. And besides, I needed to shut myself off and deal with this. I knew it was my struggle, and as always I would engage and deal with it in my own way. Very gradually the tears subsided, and the pain slowly dulled. I loved my daughter so very much, and the extreme sorrow and regret that I felt at my actions would remain with me always, another dark blot on the landscape of my life. But there are handholds, even in the deepest darkest pit, which can be reached and climbed.

Whenever life closes one door another always opens. Despite our strongest endeavours, mere humans will not thwart destiny's plans. I cancelled flights for Spain that Kate and I had arranged for our Easter break, and was wondering where else I could go, my instinct for the healing effects of the sun kicking in. Lying on the sofa one evening struggling with the Telegraph cryptic crossword, I stumbled upon my first answer: 'Aphrodite'. Cyprus! My mind raced. It was somewhere familiar. The weather would be good. But then, Leon might be there. I knew that Easter was the time for one of his regular visits. I wondered what I should do. It would be embarrassing to run into him with a new girlfriend. I wrote, explaining what had happened, that I would like to go to Cyprus but did not wish to 'cramp his style'. Perhaps we could avoid being there at the same time? The response was not what I had expected. He called me a few days later, asking when I would be arriving; date, time, etc., so that he could collect me from the airport. I rushed to explain that my feelings had not changed; I just needed a rest, some time in the sun. But he insisted. I agreed, on the strict understanding that it was on a friends only basis, and that I wanted my own space and time alone. So flights were booked, and on 6th April 1997, I flew out to Cyprus, totally unsuspecting that I was heading into a whole new phase of my life.

CHAPTER 32

Larnaka airport was heaving with people criss-crossing the small concourse, dragging trolley loads of suitcases and gifts. It was coming up to Easter and many Cypriots living in England were returning home for the celebrations. I fought my way through the mêlée towards the entrance – one set of double doors – through which all the arrivals would be cramming, and saw him, standing there head and shoulders above everyone else, anxiously peering around, searching the crowds for me. I waved, caught his attention, and he pushed his way through to me, taking my hand and the trolley at once. It was good to see him again. Outside, the late afternoon sun was still hot, and I took a moment to stand and enjoy the warm feeling of its rays on my face. The journey to the hotel was only about forty-five minutes, during which we chatted inconsequentially, generally catching up with each other's lives. He checked me in, and asked if I would like to meet for a drink before going out to dinner. Choosing to ignore his presumption that we would be dining together, I said "Yes, that would be lovely."

I spent the next hour or two in my room alternating between unpacking, and enjoying the view from my balcony. Takis was in the bar when I walked through, and welcomed me like a long lost friend. I felt that I had come home. Leon's eagerness to pick up where we had left off the previous summer was touching, and difficult to resist. But I resolved to keep our relationship on a simple, friendly basis, and to an extent he respected my wishes.

We dined together each evening, and each morning he would call to ask if I were ready for breakfast, and could he join me. I passed my days in my favourite spot, lying by the pool, reading, and left him to join me or not as he wished. Mostly, he did. Leon's room was two floors below mine, and at the end of each evening, after we had dined, and maybe danced and taken a nightcap with Takis, he would step out of the lift ahead of me, leaving me with a friendly peck on the cheek, but with a look in his eyes that clearly showed his desire for more.

Now, looking back, I can conjure up a picture of Leon, and see his tall solid frame, strong limbs, and large hands. He smiles at me with his whole face, eyes alight with joy and mouth wide, showing the tiny gap between his two front bottom teeth. I go further and imagine him holding me, enfolding me in his strong arms, holding my body close to his, which always exudes warmth. I can smell him. I can feel my small, cold hand encompassed by his; fingers seemingly short for such a tall man, but at the same time, firm, strong and soft. These sensations are so real, so vivid I hang onto them for as long as I can, at least until the tears come, and I have to let him go. Nothing has replaced the sense of safety, and well being that I felt then in his arms. So though I ask myself now what made me change my mind about the nature of our renewed friendship, and try as I might to locate a sound reason for my subsequent decision, I think the answer lies not in logical reason, but in my senses, in the base female instincts that react to the male that offers a salve to her innermost needs.

And so it was that late on the fourth or fifth night, after I had returned to my room, without conscious thought or calculated decision, I slipped into a hotel dressing gown, left my room, and tiptoed down the back stairs of the fire escape, to the third floor. As I tapped on his door, a rush of cold panic shivered through me:

What if he says, "No thank you!"

But before I had time to react and decide, the door opened, and he was standing there, in his hotel dressing gown, his face first registering surprise, but quickly changing to delight. Neither of us spoke a word as he opened the door wide, I stepped forward, and he took me in his arms.

Had I crossed the Rubicon? He wanted me in his life; I knew that, and the action I had taken that night, from his point of view, added that final missing dimension to our relationship. For me it was an expression of my commitment to him, but in the sense of an exchange of gifts. His gift to me would be priceless, but at that stage I am not sure that he had any real understanding of my neediness. He had however, commented to me during the earlier months that we had been together, that my choice of music had led him to believe that there was a great sadness in me. I had taken the first small step out across the bridge, and this move towards him freed us on all levels to enjoy each other.

We had fun together, often childish. Playing in the sea, he loved to pick me up and throw me into the waves. Our adult senses of humour fused; we were often asked why we were always laughing. And of course it was wonderful once again to have a man on my arm, especially one so handsome. And on a deeper level, he was able to heal my emotional wounds, by encouraging the child in me to show her fun side, allowing her to be natural, silly and to express spontaneity. I don't know if this was a conscious effort on his part, or just a natural progression as my trust in him grew. Slowly, slowly as the months passed I grew to believe that he would not hurt me. And for the first time in my life, I began to accept that I was loved simply because I was me. John had once told me that it would take a very special man to love me, with my complicated mix of vulnerability and stubborn strength, and in Leon I had found him. We were so very happy, very much in love with each other, making no plans for the future but just enjoying the days, or weeks that we could be together.

Though it would remain difficult for some considerable time, my relationship with Kate had not been destroyed entirely, and we did occasionally spend days together, or speak on the telephone, while she remained with Philip. In turn this gave me the space and opportunity to be with Leon as often as possible. We settled into a lifestyle that would accommodate his business commitments, along with mine. Mostly I would travel to Blackpool to stay with him in his apartment in the new hotel, and as often as possible we would go to Cyprus.

That summer was marred only by one event, which at the time appeared isolated, but which would permanently impact our life together. During our first period of courtship I had met Leon's son and daughter only once, when he had arranged for us all to have dinner together. They had both been very friendly, and I had no reason to assume that things would change. He had been separated from their mother for sixteen years, so I was not an interloper in that sense. His daughter was to be married that summer, the wedding taking place in Cyprus, in July. Leon asked me to come, and I declined, unsure that I should be involved in such an intimate family affair, so early on in our relationship. He presented me with an invitation, and all my arguments for not going were gently rebuffed – his brothers and sister in Cyprus all liked me very much and his ex-wife had decided not to go so he needed me there. Eventually, against my better judgement, I agreed to go. It was an unmitigated disaster.

By the time the wedding arrived Leon was feeling not a little exasperated with the groom's attitude. Our previous stay in Cyprus had been taken over by rushing between Limassol on the coast, and Morphu in the mountains, making last minute arrangements for the formalities required for non-Cypriots to marry in the island. And daily faxes had arrived in our hotel room from the groom demanding immediate responses to various requests.

I arrived in Cyprus to discover that his ex-wife was in fact attending the wedding. Leon collected his daughter and fiancée from the airport, and from the moment they arrived at the hotel it was quite clear that my presence was not wanted. I was treated like a pariah. With the one exception of Leon's son, all the other guests avoided me, to the extent that when I walked to the pool bar to sit and have a coffee, the groom's parents immediately left theirs behind on the bar and walked away. Leon was told that under no circumstances was I to be present at any of the pre-wedding functions, let alone the wedding, and I watched in dismay as he slowly disintegrated into a shaking wreck. Finally, one evening, seeing him literally go grey whilst listening to his daughter insisting that he should turn up to the drinks party without me, I took the phone from his hands and told her what I thought of her behaviour, though I did add that, for her father's sake, I would 'butt out' of the proceedings. I could see what his resistance to her demands was costing him and I was angry that her selfishness was placing us all in such a difficult situation. A few minutes later the groom burst into our room, grabbed me by the shoulders and threatened me with dire consequences if I did not stay away. Leon looked on, helpless, unable to intervene on my behalf, and it was left to me to stand up to this arrogant man, insisting that he leave my room or I would call hotel security.

I knew that I had to take a back seat, for Leon's sake. It was his daughter's wedding, a special time for any father, and yet he did not want to hurt me. We arranged that I would spend the wedding day with Takis and his family, not returning to the hotel until it was all over.

I returned to our room late that night. Looking out from the balcony I could see the wedding party in full swing, and a rush of old, and of late unfamiliar, feelings accosted me. I was not good enough to be a part of the group. I was not wanted. So easily tipped back into that old pattern, I began to cry, to tremble, and I felt sick, longing to be away from them all, Leon included, back in my little house where I would be safe, where I could not be abused. My bad feelings were compounded when Leon's sister and brothers came to our room to collect their belongings, and looked at me with what I took to be pity, but which was probably embarrassment. Leon came tired and late to bed, though he could see how distressed I was. He promised me that the next day, as soon as he had carried out his final few obligations, we would take off to one of our favourite haunts in the mountains.

Over a glass of wine, in peaceful surroundings, away from the awful atmosphere at the hotel, I told him how hurt I had been, and that I considered it partly his fault for insisting that I came. I explained that I understood fully, that on this occasion, he had no option but to appease his daughter, but I could never allow him to do that to me again. Though it deeply upset me to tell him this, I knew it to be true, and I knew that I could follow through, and leave him. I was jealous to protect the small sapling of self worth that had begun to grow in me, even from the man whose love had coaxed it into being. His response was comforting, and reassuring. He wanted me, I was integral to his future happiness, and his daughter must accept that. But the seed was sown; from that day there would always be one area of his life from which I would be barred. How must he have felt, being in the invidious position of having to choose between the two women who mattered most to him? Eventually when his resolve began to fail, he would deceive me; lie about why his journey home from Blackpool had taken so long.

LOVE TRIANGLE

Her selfish needs
Demanding
Clawing
Clutching
Wanting to remain
The number one
Pole position

And hers
The other woman
New woman in his life
Different from those who had been
And gone
Before
She was not a casual affair
She was a threat
She too demanded

His focus had shifted
He needed too
And she filled
And satisfied
As the first could never
Ever do

Hooking into their prey
Pulling in opposing directions
Tearing at the fabric of another life
Each claiming for her own
His body, heart and soul

Each testing her strength
Against the other
Teasing
Fighting

A ruthless battle
To possess and keep
The prize
His love
Beyond the reach
Of the other

Pitiful prey
Crouching, cowering
Petrified
He has no choice
Where his heart may lie

And yet
His needs
Cannot be fulfilled
By one
Or the other
Alone

He needs each
To hold their part
Not dividing
Nor splitting
His heart

He would not choose
Could not choose
He thinks –
No need to choose

But they will not relent
Never
This battle will ensue
Even unto his death
When he will lay between them
Care less then of their shameful self-interest
Finally at peace

Beyond their reach
Forever
At last
Content

As usual my flight back to England was a day or two ahead of his. Unusually, it was very early in the morning and for the first time since meeting him I took a taxi to the airport. He was exhausted by the three-week onslaught on his emotions, and I left him fully clothed, asleep on the bed in our hotel room, left him without saying goodbye. World events took over my sorrow though, because it was August 31st 1997, and I landed at Heathrow, to learn that Princess Diana had been killed that night in a car crash in Paris.

CHAPTER 33

The shock of Diana's death, watching the extensive news coverage of the public outpouring of emotion, as well as getting back into work, eased me through any remaining sadness that I may have felt over the last days of our holiday together.

After Leon's return to England we spoke on the telephone and he seemed his normal cheerful self, though he admitted to feeling very tired.

It was one Saturday in mid-September that my concern was aroused when I called the hotel to be told that he was unwell, and had asked not to be disturbed. I persuaded the receptionist to put me through, and asked him what was wrong. He would not be specific, just that he had a high temperature, and was staying in bed for a day or two. This was so unlike him, I offered to drive up. No, he was insistent, he would be fine in a day or two. I put the phone down, and deciding to ignore his plea to be left alone, packed my bags, which were ever ready for the journey to Blackpool, locked the house and set off, making the 260 mile journey in record time, arriving late afternoon at the hotel.

Some minutes after my knock, he opened the door of his apartment, and for the first time ever, did not look pleased to see me. And I could see why. His tousled hair from two days in bed, stale breath, flushed cheeks and sweaty pyjamas, told me something was seriously wrong. His obvious embarrassment quickly turned to relief, as he showed me the problem. His left testicle was swollen and he was in great pain. I stayed with him, took him back to the GP first thing Monday, and within hours he was in Blackpool Victoria hospital. The consultant reassured us that it was nothing more than a severe infection, but as it had not responded to the antibiotics there was now no alternative remedy other than removal. Listening to the consultant, I was also looking at Leon as this news was delivered. His face was a picture of shock and horror.

"But, what about…"

Knowing what was coming, the consultant interrupted, laughing.

"Don't worry; it won't affect your manhood. You can manage just as well with one." Leon looked at me, needing reassurance: "Sure we can!" I said.

Surgery was carried out quickly, and within a few days Leon was back at the Hotel recuperating. With the surgeon's blessing we arranged a trip to Cyprus to aid Leon's recovery. Unfortunately, within hours of arriving in Cyprus, Leon began to experience great pain in his lower abdomen, and was taken into hospital in Limassol. Luckily for me, the consultant had trained in London and spoke excellent English. He explained that there were further complications and he needed to operate. Consequently we spent most of our planned restful holiday in hospital. There were however, two positive outcomes from this episode, in that I was forced to drive the car in the busy Cypriot traffic in central Limassol, to get myself to and from the hospital, and the difficulties of communication with the nurses due to the language barrier determined a resolve in me to learn Greek.

Back in England Leon very quickly regained his health, was signed off by the surgeon and 1997 drew to a close without more problems.

On reflection I can see that 1998 was the year in which we made small, but irrevocable steps towards cementing our future together. In January, I finally persuaded Leon to come with me to Spain, hoping that he would fall in love with Duquesa as I had, and that we could enjoy the occasional holiday in Spain as well as Cyprus. He did love the apartment, who couldn't? But he did not fall in love with Spain. Although Anglicised, he was Cypriot through to his core, and if he were going to spend time in the sun, he wanted it to be in Cyprus. I could understand this, remembering how I had yearned for England, my home, when I was living in Spain.

I do not recall the order of our decisions, nor even if they were consciously linked, but within a few short weeks of returning to England, I had decided to sell the apartment in

Spain, and to move somewhere slightly further north in England so that the journey between our two homes would not be so long. Maybe because my apartment had ignited a small flame in his heart Leon started talking about buying a house in Cyprus.

In February I celebrated my 50th birthday with Leon, close friends and all three of my children at a party in The Royal Oak, next door to my cottage in old Sunningdale, almost four and one half years since I had taken the momentous decision to leave Philip. Though the ride at times had been exceedingly rough I had no regrets, no longings for anything left behind. I considered myself exceptionally lucky to have such a close group of friends to share in my celebration. I could see the road ahead, and it looked smooth, and straight.

Significantly, this was the first mid-winter in three years that I not spent time in the clinic. I still had the occasional wobble, but Leon was always there to hold me, soothe my worries, and carry me through. Worryingly, I sometimes still experienced panic – not manifested outwardly, in breathlessness or shaking, but internalised, in some inexplicable sense of fear. On rare occasions it would leave me rooted to the spot, unable to move forward. However, in the main, I had reached another plateau on my healing journey and I was enjoying this respite, bathing in Leon's love and attention. His calm had a positive influence on me, and was a perfect foil for my occasional outbursts when frustration with events exploded into anger.

By now Kate knew Leon well and had really taken to him. In the same way that I had been, she was captivated by his natural unassuming ways. He never offered her his opinion unless it was asked for, and, fast approaching seventeen, now growing into a determined and confident young woman, she greatly respected this. Superficially at least, Kate and I were in a pretty good place. My diary was full of dates and times for meeting her, collecting her from school and notes of days off school, or when she was working weekends as a waitress in our local bistro. There were deep-rooted problems, quietly bubbling and brewing within her, but these would not surface until they were forced out by a particularly difficult and unpleasant period in her young life. I was always careful not to upset her, being only too grateful that I had the opportunity to try again. It would not be until much later that I would understand that she too was careful not to upset me; not because I may become angry, but because she was afraid of tipping me over into self harm, or putting me back into the clinic. An unhealthy relationship had therefore developed with neither of us able to be open and honest about our feelings. But any relationship was better than none, and we were neither of us prepared at that stage to look too deeply.

Leon's niece was married in Nicosia on 12th July. Because they had felt embarrassed at the way I had been treated at Leon's daughter's wedding, Leon's brother and sister-in-law expressed a strong wish that I should attend with Leon; they made me feel extremely welcome and I thoroughly enjoyed myself. My own son Adam was married six days later in England, so it took some strategic planning to attend both weddings.

Whenever we were in Cyprus, we allocated time to look at property. I did not feel it my place to influence his decision on this, willingly trotting along with him to each of the viewings. I was excited at the prospect of having a house in the sun again, but conscious that he was looking to his long term plans to maybe retire there, and at that time, I felt that these might not include me. Not because I had doubts as to Leon wanting me to be a part of his future, but because I knew that I could not leave England again, certainly not permanently.

We had accumulated a selection of restaurants where we would go to eat most nights. All had wonderful locations, varying from high in the mountains, to the rooftops of tiny village houses, to overlooking a beautiful bay down by the sea. In one of our most favourite, George, an architect, and extremely talented musician, played guitar and sang along with the owner, Costas, who played bazouki. Costas had opened the taverna in a small mountain village called Lofou, and was working hard at promoting it. We grew to love this place, and Costas and his family.

George was an old friend of Leon's and was very keen for me to meet his wife Michelle, and so we planned to have lunch in Zigi, the small village by the sea, where Leon and I had eaten our last lunch together on that first holiday in Cyprus when we had met. For some reason I took an instant dislike to Michelle. This feeling was exacerbated by her behaviour, when during lunch she took great pains to remind me that Leon 'had a past' and that she knew all about it. As we were finishing our Cypriot coffees, and I was feeling relieved that we would soon be able to make our excuses and leave, she grabbed my cup and said:

"I can tell the future in these coffee grounds."

I replied, as courteously as I could, but firmly, saying that I was not interested and did not believe in such things. She insisted, tipping my cup upside down and banging the grounds onto the table. She looked at me, and then Leon.

"Well?" he said, laughing.

Her eyes returned to me, and though I knew it to be nonsense, her words stayed with me, and they were uncannily prophetic.

"This man will bring you many tears, but not because he will stop loving you."

One other occasion from that summer stands out in my memory. We were dining at Yialos – a favourite restaurant of ours in the small seaside village of Pissouri – sitting at a table on the first floor, which extended out towards the beach. The only sound was that of the waves gently washing the sand, and a golden moon hung in the sky above the promontory. Clichéd, I know, but this is exactly how it was. Quietly eating our meal, chatting about nothing in particular, Leon said,

"You never know, I might even ask you to marry me."

Without looking up from my meal, thinking he was joshing, I replied,

"Don't bother, I shan't make that mistake again!"

The silence was deafening, I looked up to see the hurt on his face, and realized, too late, that he had been testing the water. What could I say? I muttered something about it being a painful experience, and one would always need to think hard before entering that state again. I had hurt him, and felt dreadful. But it did make me think. Could I marry again? We were happy enough as we were; why marry? Certainly we would not be having children. But then, marriage is a very public statement of a commitment to someone, a promise to spend the rest of life with them, care for them through all events. Did I feel that strongly about him? Could I stand up in front of all my family and friends and make those promises, knowing that I had done so once before, and been unable to keep them?

Both of these incidences – the prophecy and the half proposal – would come crashing into my mind together at some future, as yet unknown time. Separate, unrelated at the moment of their enactment, they would unite, bringing the joy and the sorrow together to weave the path that we were destined to follow.

Towards the end of the year, everything was coming together. The apartment in Spain had sold, and we had found a beautiful house in Agios Tychonas, just west of Limassol, close to the hotel where we had first met. We both fell in love with it, on first viewing, and decided to call it "Y Foliamos" – Our Nest. Perhaps this was because because Leon had always called me "Poulakimou" – my little bird. Leon had decided to sell the large hotel that he had bought in 1996. Finding good managers was proving to be a problem, and he wanted more time away from the business, to enjoy his new house in Cyprus.

We celebrated what would turn out to be our last Christmas at The Old Forge, and 1999 spread out before us, like a veritable feast. Though my little cottage had not yet sold, we had settled into an easy and comfortable routine sharing our time together between his hotel in Blackpool, my house and Cyprus. I felt truly blessed.

CHAPTER 34

Throughout the previous eighteen months, my friendship had deepened with Dawn and Mick; the couple who had become my friends during the early days of marriage with Philip. Their house being almost exactly half way between Sunningdale and Blackpool, just off the M40 motorway, made it a very useful stop over. Occasionally I would stay overnight, but more often I would break the journey on a Friday afternoon, between 4pm and 7pm in order to avoid the horrendous traffic queues on the motorways. Initially the excuse would be that we could discuss business – she was now managing the sales for me on my two parks – but as time passed and our knowledge and understanding of each other grew we became firm friends. Mick had for many years been the big brother I had never had and was very protective towards me. I don't know if he ever even fully trusted Leon. But like all my friends, they took to his warm and friendly character, and seemed to have quietly given their blessing to our relationship.

I grew to admire and respect another aspect of Dawn's character that I had never previously been aware of, which was her intense and complete faith in God. Unlike me, she accepted biblical teaching without questioning the great and apparent implausibility in the stories of Genesis, or the Resurrection. She had an experience of God, and a deep belief in the power of prayer that was to me, enviable, powerful and yet possibly foolish in its innocent acceptance. Very often our conversation would turn to heated discussion, as my unsatisfied thirst for understanding and answers would impact her simple and resolute faith. I would challenge her, almost rudely trying to find the weakness that I suspected must be there. But I couldn't penetrate the wall of faith that surrounded her; a faith that has carried her through an immense amount of suffering and pain through both hers and Mick's years of ill health.

Almost imperceptibly my desire for understanding transformed into a yearning for the sense of peace that emanated from her. I knew that my emotions and raging were far from settled: my turbulent nature would quickly and inexplicably swing from one extreme mood of elation and joy into a deep sadness, and I wanted some of whatever it was she was on! I had yet to learn that the answer would not be found in books, or from listening expectantly to the experiences of others. I must set out along my own journey to faith – step out and trust. But could I ever fully and unreservedly trust in a man, a father figure, albeit a divine one?

Blackpool hoteliers rely to a large extent on summer visitors, despite the very variable weather. Income and tourism peaks during the period of the famous illuminations but these are switched off in late autumn, and winter revenues are essential to maintain a healthy profit and pay the staff. It was therefore a foregone conclusion that I would join Leon in Blackpool for Valentine's Day, for the two-day special event that the hotel would hold, but I had asked Leon if we could return to Sunningdale together to celebrate my birthday on the 21st.

I arrived a day or two before the 14th, to find that Leon was once again unwell. His GP had diagnosed a urinary tract infection and prescribed antibiotics. Nonetheless, his condition worsened. We returned to the doctor, who was somewhat dismissive of Leon's discomfort, and prescribed yet more antibiotics. Despite the repeated medication, there was still no improvement, and Leon began to complain that it was becoming more difficult to pee. I countered this by encouraging him to drink more, believing that this was necessary to clear the infection.

Two nights before we were due to return to Sunningdale, I awoke to the sound of violent retching. I switched on the bedside light, as Leon emerged from the bathroom, reeling. Still retching, sweating profusely, all he could utter were the words,

"Pain, awful pain".

Shocked and frightened at seeing him in such a dreadful state I telephoned the night porter on reception and asked him to call an ambulance. When he called back it was to tell me that it would be at least forty minutes before one would arrive. I dressed myself, and Leon as best I could, and called down for help to get Leon into the car so that I could take him to the hospital myself. The night porter's look of horror confirmed my belief that Leon was seriously ill.

Much later, I left him settled in the hospital, exhausted but at least more comfortable, and returned to the hotel alone. When I arrived the following morning, Leon had been transferred to a small private room, and told that he should remain in hospital to have some tests carried out. Disappointed that I would have to cancel plans for my birthday celebration I could nevertheless see the sense in getting his infection properly cleared up. Apparently, they had been quite offhand about the tests, not communicating any indication of a more serious problem, and so neither of us were remotely prepared for the terrible news that would be delivered so brutally when the results came through. The consultant arrived, unannounced, late one afternoon, followed by his registrar and the nursing sister, who took her place quietly at the end of the bed, next to me. Without preamble, cruelly and thoughtlessly he delivered his diagnosis, and in the space of a few seconds, callously destroyed all our hopes and dreams, our lives, our future together:

"Well old boy, you have cancer."

He continued, not allowing either of us time to register disbelief or shock.

"How old are you?" looking down at his notes,

"Sixty-five, oh well, never mind, it's advanced, no point in operating, but we can keep you going for a while."

I sensed rather than saw the shock on the face of the sister. I heard her sharp intake of breath, and knew that like me she was horrified at the manner in which our nemesis had been declared.

Fighting back tears, my eyes focused on Leon, I saw a flash of paralysing fear in his; saw it in that same instant that it took him to mask it, recover and replace it with his natural calm expression.

I turned on the consultant, fury overcoming my shock:

"You must have known last year, why didn't you check? Why didn't you call him back for a follow up check?"

Even my anger did not touch him. The sister quietly took hold of my arm, as he rounded on me:

"I'll speak to you later, when you've calmed down!" and, having dropped his bombshell, exited as he had entered, in flurry of white coat, clipboard and accompanying registrars, leaving the sister to pick up the pieces of devastation left behind him. She spoke softly, apologising, and then left to make some tea; that very English salve to all hurt. What else could she do?

We were left alone, staring at each other, feelings running amok, questions screaming through our heads, but more than anything, we were frightened. I couldn't lose him, not now, please not now, now that everything was finally coming good. He spoke first, and his words, coming out of such desolation, reminded me why I loved him so much, why I adored and trusted him, and was able to lean on him so often for support.

"I haven't got cancer. I can't have, I feel fine. I'll prove them wrong, and when I do we'll open a bottle of champagne."

"And if I don't, we'll open two bottles."

Later, much later, he told me that one of his first thoughts had been that I might leave him. That this was the real test of my love for him. Was I along for the fun of the journey, or was I there for the duration, whatever may come? And I recall my reply, that, coming fast on the heels of my shock was the conviction that I did want to marry him; proclaim to the world that I loved this man, so very much, and wanted to be with him, support and care for him, whatever that would mean.

And so came together the two memories from that now long ago, previous summer in Cyprus. The glorious night under the hanging moon, when Leon tentatively suggested marriage, and the prophecy held in the scattered coffee grounds, that he would bring me many tears. For the second time in two years I found myself fervently wishing that I could turn back the clock, wishing that life could take a different path from the one I was travelling along.

CHAPTER 35

My coping mechanism kicked in. Tears and anger would come later. My fighting instinct, my stubborn determination to overcome adversity would not accept that this was a death sentence. Leon was refusing to give in and I would fight for him against any odds, not accepting the prognosis, nor the suggestion that there was little that could be done. With Leon's blessing, I returned to the hotel and called my own GP, pleading with him to take Leon on. He calmed me, reassuring me that prostate cancer was not necessarily a death sentence and that there was much that could be done. We agreed that I should bring Leon home to Sunningdale, and that he would arrange a private appointment with a local man who was extremely well respected in this field.

Leon discharged himself from the hospital, we packed, made arrangements that were necessary for the management of the hotel, and returned home to Sunningdale. As far as the staff were concerned Leon was coming back with me to rest and recuperate. True to his word my GP had arranged for us to see the specialist in Windsor within a few days. A different man, caring and concerned, he did tell us that the cancer was advanced, but that he would operate, and try to remove it. He explained the procedure, and that if the cancer had not spread beyond the shell of the prostate, the future looked positive. Privately, he told me that he feared this might not be the case. Surgery was planned for Thursday 4th March 1999.

Initially, Leon's great strength and refusal to admit his cancer was a powerful antidote to any low feelings that we may have experienced. His way of dealing with the cancer was to deny its very existence and I had to show strength and resolution to match his. But my way was not through denial. I needed to talk, ask questions, understand my enemy in order the better to fight it. I needed to offload my fears and anger; my tears needed release. And so we started out along our separate journeys, needing to fight this war both united as one force, but also engaging in our own very necessary private battles. Coming together in strength, but separating for much needed respite from the continuous strain of being strong and positive.

Eileen, the lovely Christian lady who had taught Katie the piano, and subsequently become my close friend, was now living in a quiet cul-de-sac in Chobham, not two miles from the hospital. Her home, still a wonderful oasis of peace, was my first stop after leaving Leon the night before his surgery. I knew Dawn was visiting her, and we had planned to spend the evening together. With them I was able to release the bottleneck of emotions that had been building those past ten days. My tears flowed copiously as they prayed, holding onto me, encouraging me to tell God how I felt. And I did, boy how I did. Shouting at Him, telling Him how unfair this was, asking Him why? Why had He done this to us? Eileen and Dawn continued to pray through my anger, not stopping until, for the first time, I prayed to Him, not perfunctorily as I did in church, following the ritualised pattern, but from my heart, begging Him, pleading with Him.

"Please Lord, please give us more time. I know you can if it is Your will. Please Lord, even just five more years."

Why did I ask for five years? Did I fear that a request for too much would stand no chance of being granted? I have no idea. The words flowed without thought, through my tears, but I do recall a sense that five years would last forever. A simple prayer, unconsidered in its implication, coming from someone desperate for help, calling on an unknown higher authority, in a moment of deep need. But this prayer, uttered and then stored away in my memory, would resurface in time – chilling, shocking, but nevertheless affirming my growing belief in the power and love of an Almighty God.

I arrived at the hospital the following morning in time to see Leon before he went into surgery. He was of course nervous, but keen to have the procedure over. Whilst he was in theatre, I waited in his room, willing the consultant surgeon to return and tell me, what? I wished for a good outcome, but knew the chances were slim. The wait was longer than I had been led to expect, so my fears increased in line with the lengthening time. When the surgeon appeared in the doorway, I looked at him, hopefully, expectantly, and fearfully.

"I cannot believe I'm telling you this, but it looks as though we have caught it just in time. I was sure we were too late."

Overjoyed, relief flooding through me, I threw my arms around his neck in gratitude. Leon was going to be fine. Did I stop to thank God? Probably, in passing, as we all do. But not down on my knees, as I should have done, thanking Him from my heart. I took his gift and moved on, grateful but quickly convincing myself that this was meant to be, would have been the outcome regardless of our prayer, still doubting His existence.

We were told that radiotherapy would be necessary as a belt and braces exercise, but that the prognosis was good. Leon could look forward to many more years of life. We did open a bottle of champagne, and just for the hell of it, a second one!

The following months were dominated by the routine of post-operative treatment; a three-month course of drugs followed by radiotherapy, which took up almost every day for six weeks, and the difficulties of running the hotels from long distance. Despite this, we still managed to find time to look at properties in the Cotswolds, and South Warwickshire, the two areas that I had settled on as being closer to Blackpool, but not too far from my own businesses and my children.

One Thursday morning in late May, Kate and I were returning to Sunningdale – having stayed overnight in Birmingham after a concert at the NEC – and decided to take a detour to look at a house in a small village in Welford on Avon, Warwickshire. As I had suspected, the house was not at all what I was looking for, but Kate noticed one a little further along the road that had a 'For Sale' sign outside. It looked perfect, and peeping on tiptoe to look over the wall, we saw a beautiful lawned garden. To one side there were open fields, and to the other an old farmhouse and converted stable block, again surrounded by open fields. We made an appointment to view the house on the following Saturday morning. Leon had returned to Blackpool after the concert, and so Kate and I drove up to Welford, both very excited, early on the Saturday morning. As soon as we walked through the front door I knew this was the one, and Kate, destroying all my bargaining power in one sentence, excitedly proclaimed;

"Oh Mummy, this is so you, it's just perfect."

The sale was quickly agreed as the owners wanted to purchase a house at auction in June. Contracts were exchanged 19th June, whilst Leon and I were in Cyprus. He had not even seen it! We could not move until late August when Leon had completed his radiotherapy course, but as the owners had moved out in July we did manage a couple of visits, both of which confirmed in my mind that this was indeed 'the one'.

August soon came and our joy at moving into the new house was doubled, when, on our final visit to the consultant we were told that Leon was 'cured' and that we should go away and enjoy the rest of our lives together. I don't recall who first raised the subject, or whether we just slipped into discussion of the future we now had, but it was soon after moving into Welford that we decided to get married. It was my son Adam who, to Leon's delight, suggested a Cypriot wedding, and so towards the end of that year we began making plans to be married in Cyprus in June 2000. My doubts that friends from England would not be able to come were soon swept away by the positive responses to our invitations.

Once again, the future was looking very rosy. Our wedding took place on 3rd June 2000, at our favourite taverna in Lofou, where Costas and George sang. It had been an easy choice for us, and proved popular with our English guests. I took a course of Greek dancing lessons, determined to dance at our wedding in a manner befitting the culture of our venue, and my mastery of the Greek language had progressed enough for me to make a small speech, albeit with Leon's youngest brother Kakos, standing at my shoulder, anxiously marking my every word. Our love sealed, our future secured, and this momentous occasion shared with our families and closest friends, we could not have been happier. We passed the remainder of that summer happily drifting between our new home in Welford, and Cyprus; our 'honeymoon', a cruise from Los Angeles, through the Panama to the Caribbean being planned for September.

One black cloud did send a shiver down my spine in the autumn of 2000. My brother Tony and his wife had come to our wedding. We had not been close since childhood; both of us pretty much getting on with our own lives, and though he knew about my abuse at the hands of our father, we never talked about it. He had married young like me, but his marriage to a lovely, bubbly girl, Ann had survived the test of time, and they were still very much in love with each other. I don't recall the catalyst for our renewed relationship, but since I had known Leon we had started to see each other again and despite the distance between us geographically, we made an effort to meet up regularly. The four of us got on very well, Ann and Leon particularly forming a close bond. The day they left Cyprus after the wedding, standing in the gardens of the hotel, saying goodbye, Ann said to me "I don't want to go". Later she remembered these words and told me that it was almost as though she had a premonition. In October of that year, we had a telephone call from Tony telling us that Ann had been diagnosed with breast cancer. She was forty-six. I was devastated. I did not want to accept that another dear and loved person would have to battle this awful disease.

Because You're a Woman

Because you are a woman
You know the joy
Of that beautiful moment
Ever remembered
When
Your body gives life
To another being

The pain of birth
Instantly forgotten
With the surge
Of the first suckle
Drawing life
From your very core

Because you are a woman
You know the joy
Of watching your child
Take his first few steps
Speak her first few words
Your heart held still
Your hands ready
To catch
Less he should fall
Or stumble

Because you are a woman
You remember always
The pain of parting
On his first day at school
On her last day at home

Because you are a woman
You can love a man
With passion

And strength
With tears
And with joy

Because you are a woman
You have fought
For those you love
Your son
Your daughter
Your man

Defended and protected them
With all your might
Against all foe
And all the trials
That life has brought them

And now

Because you are a woman
You will fight for yourself
With all your strength
And all your will

For this new enemy
Unseen
Through you also attacks
Your son
Your daughter
Your man

Because you are a woman
You will win.

For Ann, 18ᵗʰ October 2000.

CHAPTER 36

August Bank Holiday, 2000, we were strolling around the Welford fete with Mick and Dawn, when she took my arm and pointed to a large marquee sitting in one corner of the field, saying words to the effect; "There, you've been asking questions for too long, now it's time to find some answers". A big banner hanging over the entrance proclaimed 'Alpha Course'. And so, a few weeks later, I found myself along with fourteen others, starting a twelve week programme advertised as an introduction to the Christian faith, but one which attempts to answer such questions as, 'Why did Jesus die?' and 'How does God guide us today?' Since moving into the village I had been to the church in Welford, as I thought this would be a good place to start meeting people: so some of the faces were familiar. I enjoyed the course immensely; my thirst for answers and knowledge being satisfied to some degree, but at the same time intensified. I believed that Jesus had lived, and that He was a great teacher, but the crux of the whole story hangs on the resurrection. Either He was resurrected and was the Son of God, or He was simply a great teacher. The arguments for the resurrection were very persuasive, but to accept them would mean that there is a God and that He had created the world. This was a step too far for me. But it was also obvious to me that the Christians leading the programme had found the same inner peace and conviction as Dawn. These were intelligent, thinking people. What had they discovered that had so dramatically changed their lives? For they would freely admit that it was God who had changed their lives. My curiosity, added to my need to 'prove' beyond doubt that what they were saying was true led me to read more. I tried to find faith through pages of text, frustrating myself even further when it didn't come. I read and reread the passage in Revelations that says: 'Behold, I stand at the door and knock. If anyone hears My voice, and opens the door, I will come in to him...' But, try as I might the understanding that I wanted remained tantalisingly close, but unattainable. I had a persistent vision of trying to find this 'door'. I retain a vivid picture, a sense of running the length; backwards and forwards, of a long and high wall, knowing that there was a door in it somewhere, but I was unable to find it. I remember something Fritz said to me once during one of our hurried conversations when I told him that I was leaving Philip, but was frightened at the prospect of being alone. He said;

"Let go, and I will catch you if you fall."

This is what God was waiting for me to do, but I was a long way from having the trust and faith to hand my life over to Him. Life was too perilous and unpredictable and I needed to hold onto control of mine.

Kate, who was now nineteen and grown into a beautiful young woman, had brought her current boyfriend to our wedding. She had not known him long, but already they seemed very much in love. I knew that Leon had his doubts about the young man because he had communicated to me his surprise at some remarks that he had made about Kate once when they were alone together in the car. He was charming and though I had no reason at the time not to like him, I was concerned that Kate appeared very jittery around him, and that she had lost a lot weight. Of course, she looked stunning being so tall and slim, but I could sense that something was not right. Perhaps she had met her 'Fritz'? My intuition turned out to be correct, and the relationship ended dramatically a few short weeks later. It was not until later the following year that I learned how abusive their relationship had been. Nevertheless, she moved on, started a new job, and met a new man, Chris, who lived in Banbury. To all outward appearances she was extremely happy.

My relationship with Kate had not improved from the tentative, tiptoeing around each other that we had settled for, and at times this created a very difficult atmosphere. Over-sensitive about each others moods, we would always be asking if anything was wrong, knowing that the answer "No", was not true, but unwilling to press further.

In January 2001 she confided in me that she was self-harming. She explained, tearfully, that she would provoke an argument with Chris, and when it rose to fever pitch she would lock herself in the bathroom and claw her arms until they bled. I was shocked, and immediately fearful that this was a result of her childhood trauma, of her parents' marriage break-up. I persuaded her to see a counsellor, and through my old contacts was able to locate one near where she lived in Banbury. There were issues from her childhood that she needed to explore and discuss, but there were also problems resulting from the abusive relationship from which she had so recently escaped. Those, however, are part of her story, not mine.

After several sessions, she called and advised me that her counsellor had suggested a meeting with her father, and myself, explaining that there were things she needed to say to us, but in a safe and controlled environment. My reaction was defensive. What was she going to accuse me of? I tackled her about this meeting, trying hard to discover what it was she needed to say so that I could prepare my defence. But she refused to discuss anything. She stuck rigidly to her line that it was best left until we were all together. She tried to reassure me, saying that it would be all right, that I would not be under attack. I could see that she was following the advice of her counsellor, rightly waiting until the planned meeting, but I desperately needed to protect myself. I was very frightened of walking into a situation for which I was not prepared, and which I sensed could well cause me a great deal of pain and grief. I could have refused to go. But my own bitter experiences had taught me that childhood trauma left to fester created untold problems in adulthood. I still felt immense guilt at breaking up the family home, and at my treatment of her that fateful Mothers' Day. I knew that I could not let my daughter down again. For the sake of her future, her children and our long-term relationship I had to go through with this. Nevertheless, my insecurities and guilt complex took control and I approached the session with great anxiety.

There were two women counsellors present, as well as Philip, myself, and Kate. I sensed, probably mistakenly, that Kate's regular counsellor did not like me; that she judged me as a bad mother, and despite efforts made to make me feel comfortable, I decidedly did not. I found the session challenging, I felt alone and under attack. Kate needed to tell me how angry she was at the way I had treated her, the time when I had rapped her knuckles, the numerous times that I had shouted at her about homework, and she reminded me that I had once shut her in the small cupboard outside the kitchen because I was so angry with her. She was right, I had, because my anger had boiled over to such an extent that I was almost out of control and I feared that I would hit her. My anger, the repressed anger that should have been directed at my parents, had poured out onto my daughter. The chain reaction from my childhood abuse had been passed onto the next generation. I had to find the strength to stop it from passing through to the next; my grandchildren.

Philip was told that he too had let her down badly, that he should have been around more to support both of us during those bad years. But Philip's resilience in the face of accusation, and ability to hide any emotion that he may be feeling, carried him through the session, and to all outward appearance he was unaffected by any of Kate's remarks.

Tearful and angry, I tried to defend myself. I had done my best; I was not a bad mother. The second counsellor tried to offer me comfort: they were not accusing me of being a bad mother; it was just that Kate needed to tell us how angry she was about her treatment. Of course I should have seen that this was so very true. Kate was doing exactly what I had so badly needed to do but not been allowed to. But I was too far gone along the road of self-reproach to think clearly.

Guilt and shame took up residence once again in my heart, this time not over activities that I had been involved in as a child, but over my mothering of Kate. The meeting had been crafted for Kate's needs, not mine or her father's. She did thank me and tell me how important it had been for her to be able to say how she felt, but the cost to me had been high. I was distraught over the hurt that I had so unintentionally caused my daughter. Like my own mother I had been guilty of brushing it aside in the pursuit of my own life. Kate's reassurance that she felt a load had been lifted from her, and that she did love me, went only a little way to help me feel better. However, I felt that we had lifted the lid of our own Pandora's box and peeped in. Perhaps we should open it up and see what else was there?

So later in the summer, Kate and I had a few sessions together with the same two counsellors. Taken from a different stance, where I now felt on an equal footing, we were both able to express our feelings honestly and openly within this safe environment. We worked hard, and our relationship slowly but increasingly improved. At the end, the two counsellors told us what an amazing experience it had been for them to watch mother and daughter working through their problems with such determination and courage.

On August bank holiday 2001, I made a picnic with Kate's favourite things, and took her to Dover's Hill, high above Chipping Campden. It was a lovely sunny day, and the views were stunning. We enjoyed our picnic, and then we lay on the blanket together in the warm sunshine, and starting from scratch, this time being able to turn the clock back, I taught her how to do 'long division'.

"Oh Mum, is that all? It's so simple!"

CHAPTER 37

Following a routine test in late 2001 we were told that Leon's cancer had returned, and that he should take a new drug to prevent it from spreading. The drug would keep him alive, but medically castrate him. Implicit in this news was a choice, not a difficult one, but the implications on our relationship were very tough on Leon. Almost imperceptibly at first he began to withdraw from me. Still needing his arms around me, I would snuggle up to him but less and less he drew me in, and more often would, albeit gently, hold me away. I tried to draw on our ability to laugh at situations, and having found an entry in my diary, in his handwriting, saying '8.00pm live football England V Greece', followed by three exclamation marks; I wrote underneath, '10.00pm, live sex England V Cyprus' followed by three question marks. And laugh we did, but his inability to be a man, in his terms, was slowly but surely sucking the lifeblood from our relationship.

The new drug, however did not hold the cancer as well as had been hoped, and a body scan the following spring showed that the cancer had spread to Leon's spine. His consultant told me that I could only count on a year. By Christmas 2002 he was in terrible pain, and yet refused to take relief as in his eyes this acknowledged his illness, and a weakness. He started to talk about going to Cyprus, on his own, and though this hurt me, I had to accept that he needed to fight this final battle his way. Major surgery on his spine was necessary to prevent him becoming wheelchair bound, and it was after he had recovered from this, that I arrived home from shopping one day to find he had packed all his belongings and was waiting for his son to collect him. He told me he wanted to spend a couple of weeks with his children. But as we kissed goodbye, I saw the tears in his eyes, and I knew he would not be coming back. I recalled the time three weeks previously when we had laughed as I struggled to get his socks and shoes on and he had said "Oh, I love you so much". What had happened in those three weeks? Cancer had happened. Cancer had finally destroyed our relationship; not our love, but our relationship.

THE CLEVEREST GENERAL

The cleverest general
Builds his army
Quietly
Secretly
Collecting his weapons
Selecting his weapons
His troops grouping and forming
Into a fighting mass
Dark and menacing
Evil in its intent
To destroy

A slow and steady advance
Smaller cohorts
Ready at the first sign of a setback
To break away
Open another front
Forcing the unwary quarry
To bring in reserves
Some untested
As yet untried against this determined enemy

Dividing and conquering
He presses home his advance
Each pocket of resistance slowly but inevitably
Overcome

It is only a matter of time
Precious time
Time in which
If luck holds out
A new legion may arrive
Delivering a new weapon
To aid the wavering, desperate prey
Waiting, holding on

Grimly refusing to surrender

A blow is struck
And
The cleverest general staggers
The quarry recovers
A brief respite ensues
And the eye shifts
Gazing longingly
Away from the battlefield
Back to the distant green and hazy mountains in the country
of peace

But the cleverest general
Is ever cunning and remorseless

Whilst the quarry rests
Dreaming of a spring of fresh new growth
Exposing its tender underside
Lowering its barriers

Like a Trojan horse
He infiltrates
And strikes
Brutally
Violently
And the fatal blow
Is delivered

The cleverest general
Has no care that
In victory
He loses too
His reason for existence is destruction
His goal
Has been achieved
The desecration complete
Final and irrevocable
A life taken

In the event, he stayed with his daughter and within two weeks I received a cruel letter, demanding a divorce, and telling me that he was returning to Cyprus. I read it in shock, unbelieving that Leon could say such things to me. I could sense his daughter's hand in this but what could I do? I tried to call him, but was not allowed to speak to him except once, briefly, when all he would say was he needed a break, and would be going to Cyprus within two days for an indefinite period.

My mind raced to find a reason for his sudden rejection of me. What had I done wrong? What had I not done for him? His passion had subsided, along with his natural male impulses, but through all our travails we had still laughed together. I had nursed him through the surgery and recovery period, had stood by him through all the heartache of scans, treatments and hospital visits. I was desolate, inconsolable. How could he destroy all that we had? Struggling for comprehension, I closed myself away from friends and family, sinking once again into that deep pit where the darkness surrounds me, and I can just float in my own pain, and wait in hope that in time it will ease.

THIS TIME

This time
A different man
A new man
A man who loves me
Respects me
Cares for me

A man who loves me for me
For the unique mix of chemistry that I am
For the being that I am

And with the release of past hurts
And the knowledge of a new kind of love
Comes relaxation
Comfort
And a feeling of safety
And permanence

And I bask in the warm glow of this new love

But he leaves
Suddenly – gone
No warning
No time to take breath

Shattering my cosy world

His rejection tears away the fabric
Of the newfound wrap of happiness
Of dreams dared to be spoken
Shared and floated on the hopes
Of a new beginning

Tears and guilt rush in together
Self-doubt and fear filter through

The fine mesh of my newfound confidence

I ask the inevitable questions
Why?
What did I do wrong?

This time was right
This time was good
I thought

But

This time it is different
Previous pain was conquered
And I know the dark pool into which I sink
Is not too deep,
The sucking quicksand of gloom
Not so strong
As to render escape nigh impossible

This time
I can struggle myself
Start to pull upwards towards the light

Where strong hands reach down to me
And my will reaches up
And they clasp it
Firmly

I rest in their embrace
Quietly, calmly
Separate from the real world
Understanding that – for a while
I can be still and at peace
Wrapped in their cocooning love

There is no hurry
No need to struggle impatiently

I know I will survive

The light is there
A new beginning
Even if I cannot see it
Yet

Daily I trip and stumble
I cry
I grieve
I wait for the anger
Which I know must surface
Eventually through my tears of sorrow
And once this anger is spent
I will move on

This time
Wiser
Stronger

Some old friends, Ruth and Geoff, were collecting Geoff's sister who lived in Leamington and decided to call in on me for coffee. They found me still in bed, listless, unable to talk coherently. Dear Ruth, refusing to leave me alone, asked me to come home with them for a few days. I didn't want to, preferring to stay at home, feeling more comfortable in my own surroundings, able to be and feel as miserable as I wished. But she insisted, telling me that she would feel so guilty if she left me as I was, and I relented. I stayed with them for five days. Understanding that I had to work through my sorrow, they left me to rest in comfy seats in the garden – the weather had decided to be kind to us – or in their conservatory with a plentiful supply of jigsaw puzzles. I didn't do much thinking that week. My need was for some balm to soothe my aching heart.

Returning home, I was calmer and knew that I had to begin a journey away from Leon, and on to whatever the future held, though for many months my mind searched for answers that I would not receive. I could only guess at his reasons. His coping mechanism was in his denial of the illness. Living with me was a constant reminder of it. No longer able to feel desire or make love to me as he once could, with the additional physical disability following the operation to rebuild his spine, I had become his nurse; a situation that he did not want, and once he could walk again, did not need. A proud man, he needed to move away from this daily onslaught, forcing him to accept that our life together had changed irrevocably: he, no longer the strong half of the relationship, no longer the dominant alpha male. Turning away from me, moving back to Cyprus, he could live once again on the beach, in the sea and believe that he would be well again.

I did see him later in the year, when I responded to a call from him to come visit him in Cyprus. But before then I was to change. I was about to undergo an experience that would heal, comfort and strengthen me to such an extent that, when I did arrive in Cyprus in October, I was not the same woman that Leon had left in May.

Part 5: Jacki

CHAPTER 38

In July, Dawn persuaded me to spend a week with her at Lee Abbey, a Christian retreat centre, situated in the most delightful location perched above a beautiful private bay in North Devon. Almost magical, like Camelot, it has a special vitality all of its own. We arrived late afternoon, at the end of a bright sunny day and our first view of the Abbey and its grounds, set in a small valley above the coastline was breathtaking. Luckily we had been allocated a third floor room with open views down to the sea.

The days were relatively structured, but attendance at the various worship sessions, or teaching seminars was by no means compulsory. The Abbey could simply be used as a holiday break, time to be alone relaxing and enjoying the scenery. I had no preconceptions about my time there, having decided to 'suck it and see' as far as the teaching and worship went. But a look into my diary for that first evening tells the tale.

"Theme for the evening – quiet time: 'Be still for I am God', this is a very special place, restful, quiet and somehow magical…"

By the time I went to bed at the end of that first day I was hooked, and wanting to experience everything that the Abbey and its community had to offer.

On the third evening we all gathered on the small private beach for a bonfire and hot chocolate, and to watch the sun as it slowly sank into the sea on the western horizon. I was restless, sensing as I used to when I was a child, that I was somehow different from the others. I so wanted to find the peace in God that many of them appeared to have, but I was still fearful of Him. If I jumped, would He catch me, or would He let me fall? There was only one way to find out.

I held a view of myself that I judged to be pretty accurate. Leon's love had freed me to be myself. Its influence, his loving me simply because I was me, and his encouragement to be more relaxed about life had been powerful, and had had a significant effect on my constant need to look my best, allowing me to begin to understand that I could be accepted for whom I was rather than how I looked. In becoming more comfortable with myself, less needful of putting on a public persona; an outer shell of smart clothes, make-up and perfectly coiffed hair, I think I had developed a softer nature, and I noticed that people were more friendly towards me. Perhaps I had become more approachable? I had been confident that I was important to Leon, that our love for each other was equally given and the fruits equally shared; a new experience for me. Despite his inexplicable decision to leave me, these positive effects remained fairly well entrenched, and anyway, I could rationalise that his illness was probably at the root of his uncharacteristic behaviour. I knew that I was a perfectionist, and demanded high standards both of myself, and those I loved, so I was not an easy person to live with.

Despite these positive effects on my life, I still had ingrained a very negative self-image. Though I was no longer a simmering pot of repressed anger, I still needed ultimate control over my life, and unexpected hitches in my plans could still cause furious outbursts. I still carried guilt over my treatment of Kate during those years long ago when I had begun my first therapy sessions, and a conviction that in some ways I had been a bad mother. And I know, that despite all the therapy and release of much of the anger and grief, I felt bitter over my lost childhood. My perception was still of a deep well of blackness within me that had a physical presence, as though however hard I had scrubbed up the outside, the inside would still be dirty; like the rotten core in an outwardly healthy apple. How can you let anyone get really close to you, when you believe that there is a darkness that they may uncover? How close had I allowed Leon? While striving to overcome our fears of his cancer, the development and deepening of our relationship that would have come with the passing of time, had been put on hold.

How could I ever rid myself of this blackness, this rotten core that encapsulated all my negative feelings about me as a person? These feelings would always be laying in wait for an unexpected jibe or thoughtless remark, at which they would rise up and throw my emotions into disarray, destroying the calm and order that I had achieved. Could I find peace, could I ever look forward to a calmer life?

The next day an American teacher led the morning session. He told us the story of a house, and two housemaids, who were under strict orders to keep it clean and tidy for the master. But they were lazy, and one day, not expecting the master to call, decided to skip a couple of the rooms. Unexpectedly, their master turned up, and asked to look over the house. They proudly showed him the rooms that they had cleaned. But he wasn't interested, he wanted to see the other rooms, the ones that remained locked. At this point I began to weep, and as the story continued, with the master insisting that he had the keys to all the rooms in the house, I cried and cried, silently, copious tears running down my cheeks. My shoulders heaved as I tried vainly to regain control. Dawn, sitting next to me, took my hand in hers squeezing it reassuringly, trying to let me know that it was all right to cry. Suddenly, I knew why I couldn't find the door in that wall, the one I had been searching for, for so long. God wanted the keys to all my rooms, even the dark and dirty ones.

Later on, after lunch, I took a walk alone up the winding path, through the woods to the top of the outcrop where a small seat had been placed, looking over the edge of the cliff out across the swelling and rolling waves. I sat there contemplating who I was, and where I was going. I watched the sea gradually turn grey as the sun disappeared behind some clouds. A shiver ran through me. I was quite alone, and felt as though I could have been the only person alive in the world. I put all my thoughts out towards God, visually, looking away across the sea, towards the distant horizon, where sea and sky join, where heaven and earth may meet.

"Here I am Lord. Take me, come into my life and give me Your peace."

I spoke these words aloud, almost shouting them out across the vast expanse of sea and sky before me. I sat still and waited. Nothing happened. No clap of thunder, no voice from

303

above. No rush of wind or rustling of leaves in the trees behind me. Feeling somewhat dejected I walked slowly back to the Abbey.

The following day was our last and so the traditional communion service was held in the round room. We were moving towards the end of the service, and the chaplain was calling on Jesus, "Come Holy Jesus come". As he spoke these words repeatedly, I had a sense of the room closing in, that the chaplain and I were the only two in the room. My legs felt weak, and convinced that I was about to faint, I sat down on my chair. But the feeling that I was drifting away from my physical body persisted. Determined not to lose control, I fought against this strange feeling, my hands clinging tightly on to the sides of my chair. But my determination was to no avail compared to the power against which I struggled. As though hit by a broom handle, my legs were knocked from under me, and I fell forward, collapsing onto the floor. I could not speak and my body may as well have been disconnected from my brain for I could not move neither arms nor legs. I sensed movement around me, and heard a woman's voice speaking softly, telling me she was reading from Psalm 139. Tears rolled down my cheeks and I sobbed softly and continuously. Then began what I can only describe as a sense of something reaching down deep into me, something light and clean, soft and gentle, and yet powerful and unstoppable, reaching down and emptying the well of blackness. It was as though my dark rooms were indeed being cleaned out. I felt no fear, I felt cocooned in love, the anaesthetic that would relieve the pain of this surgery. I had no idea of the passage of time; I just knew that I didn't want this intense feeling of being bathed in love to stop.

Outside the house, below a small wall across the drive, was a large tree whose spreading branches provided shade from the hot July sun. After eating a late lunch, Dawn and I lay beneath this wall on a blanket for the whole afternoon, alternately sleeping and waking, sometimes chatting briefly. I think she too, had been exhausted by my experience.

Cynics will argue that I was suffering from a form of mass hysteria, or that I induced the feelings myself because I had such a strong wish to believe in God, or even that I brought the healing on myself by some super mind effort. I am not the fainting type, having only fainted once in my life upon getting out of bed too quickly after the birth of my second child. I have seen religious fervour, preachers whipping up a congregation to such a pitch that there were many 'falling down in the Spirit'. I know beyond doubt that the quiet man who was preaching was not whipping us up into hysterical reactions. I fought against what was happening, mentally and physically. I was still unsure about the nature of God; I questioned His existence, I had tested Him the day before on the cliff top, and nothing had happened. In reality the thought that such a powerful Being could actually exist terrified me. And yet, I will grant that I envied the peace of those of who did believe. If indeed my own mind had effected the transformation, the removal of the dreadful darkness within me, why then? Why not when I had been stronger and happier, when Leon was still with me? Why not at some time during the many years of therapy? Why choose that particular day and time? I don't believe that my mind alone could effect such a powerful transformation, so immediately.

Take from it what you will. Each of us needs a belief system; for some it is even a belief in nothing. But I have no doubt that God touched me that day. And I know that since that profound and wonderful experience I have no longer felt dirty inside.

So, following Leon's telephone call, I flew to Cyprus in October 2003. He had become thinner, his handsome face looking gaunt. But then he had fallen the night before I arrived, and broken his arm; maybe the first outward sign that the disease was steadily eating away at his bones. His right arm in a sling, he told me that he was pleased that I had arrived at such a fortuitous time, able to drive him out to our favourite places for dinner. I stayed in the hotel, not at our house with him. I could see from the curious look that he gave me the day we first met in the hotel lobby that he detected a change in me. The great release that I had felt inside had also manifested itself in my appearance and attitude. I strolled over to him, pecked him on each cheek, and sat opposite him, at the small coffee table. Cool, calm and collected.

Did I still love him? I cared about him, very much, but love, I cannot say. His rejection of me the previous May, his fruitless search for the life that was to be no more, his cruel letter demanding a separation, all had chipped away at my love. And of course, my pride – that vain and destructive trait that we all carry but are loath to own – would not allow me to open my heart to him once more. In a way that perhaps only I could perceive, he had abused me, and I could not allow the abuse to remain unacknowledged. Not again. I still needed explanations, but he refused to discuss his actions. He wanted to close the door on the recent past, said that I should forgive and forget. Come and stay with him in Cyprus. He wanted to move on, or was it really that he wanted to move back? To return to the carefree time when we first met in Cyprus, when our life together was just one long holiday. B.C. Before Cancer, before the drugs that he needed to take to stay alive, medically castrated him, took away his manhood and turned him into a eunuch. How can a man so vigorous, and sexually alive cope with such a fate?

CHAPTER 39

On Friday March 19th, 2004, five years almost to the day after I had prayed to God to save him, to give us just more five years, I received a telephone call from Leon's nephew in Nicosia, telling me that Leon had died at 9.30 that evening. Less than three months before his 70th birthday, the cancer had finally conquered his willpower, and won the long and arduous battle against this strong and determined opponent.

I flew to Cyprus for the funeral on March 23rd. My daughter came with me, offering the support I so badly needed to face his family. How would I be received, the wife who neglected him in his dying months? I believed that only one member of the family knew the truth, and whilst she had been understanding, admitting that Leon had been extremely difficult, how could I know what, if anything, she had told his other brothers and sister? Would their strong family ties, their Cypriot culture, bind them together leaving me as the outsider, or would I still be welcome as the new sister-in-law, a family member united with them in grief?

Somehow, seeing him lying in his coffin, looking like a waxwork dummy from a Madame Tussaud exhibition, was not the shock I had expected. After all, I had been preparing myself for this moment for two years. I cannot say that he looked calm, or at peace. He was no longer there. Leon had passed on, maybe to his own Elyssian fields. My brave, strong, youthful and sun-tanned Olympian had lain in a hospital bed in Nicosia for two months, his athletic body wasting away to a thin, pale skeleton of the man I had loved for seven passionate and exciting years.

The service in the Orthodox Church, like our marriage ceremony four years before, was sung and spoken in ancient Greek. I stood with his children and close family trying to concentrate and understand the lengthy talk given by a leader from the Cypriot Athletic Society, full of praise for one of their famous athletes, chosen for the Melbourne Olympics in 1956, winner of the triple jump and high jump for the pan

Balkan games in 1955. Finally, standing centre stage for the formal handshake with every member of the congregation I felt like a voyeur, as though this was not a part of my real life. The perspex, top section of the coffin lid allowed everyone to peer in at him, and they all did, as they slowly walked around the dais to shake our hands and offer condolences. How he would have hated it, been so angry at his weakness and frailty in succumbing to the illness, being on show for all to see like some ghastly peep show at the circus. Then it was over, a copy of the death certificate handed to me through the car window by my brother-in-law, and the short drive to the cemetery.

Tightly packed with mostly large ornate headstones, the cemetery was short on standing room, particularly around the newly dug grave. I stood to one side to allow his daughter and son to view the coffin being lowered unsteadily into the deep hole. The clear lid had been removed for the priest to perform the last rites and anoint the body with oil, but far from the pomp and ceremony of the church service, the internment was speedy and perfunctory, and the lid too hastily replaced, not straight, not tightly fitted, before the earth was shovelled into the six-foot grave. Shocking to think of the soil filling his mouth and nostrils, choking him even in death. There was an almost unseemly rush to fill the hole with earth, helping hands taking turns at the shovel. I did not know whether to laugh or cry. Feeling as though I was not a part of the scene, almost viewing from a different time and space, I was able to see and feel beyond my own grief and know that as well as ritualistic, solemn, and saddening, this act of burial was indeed just a means of disposing of a used body, no longer needed by its owner who, God willing, would exchange it for a new and better conditioned model in the promised afterlife.

Those desperate for the relief of a cigarette stood back and puffed hungrily, looking guiltily around at the rest of us as polite words were exchanged. Someone made the first move, and we all followed, moving in small quiet groups to the waiting cars. Goodbye Leon, my darling.

The family gathered at the home of my beautiful Cypriot sister-in-law, who offered tea and cakes. They were all very kind, making me promise to visit them and keep in touch. A promise I knew I would probably not keep. Would I ever return to Cyprus? Like Leon, I wished fervently that I could turn back the clock and relive those first four wonderful years. Wishful thinking – dwelling in the past is easier than facing the future.

We returned to England the following day, and left alone at home, the finality of his death, the end of our love, left me despairing of the trials of our lives. Another chapter had closed, and I had to move on. But my new challenge, my future, was all ready and waiting in the wings.

I cannot say exactly when it had begun to develop, but over the months following Leon's departure to Cyprus, there had grown in me a strong determination to set up a charity that would help other women who had suffered childhood sexual abuse. I knew how debilitating and devastating the long term effects were, and I had a sense that I had been very fortunate in the network of people who had supported me; people who had come alongside me through my different struggles, and in effect carried me through. Perhaps, in some small way I could do this for other women. I talked to Dawn and Kate, who in particular was very much aware of the damage caused, and they very quickly became enthused about the project. It was therefore, at the end of July in 2003 that 'Women for Change' was born. We met with other women working with survivors, or women who were survivors themselves and we very soon came to realise that there is a very great need for support, as well as a lack of awareness of this issue amongst the general population.

CHAPTER 40

Following Leon's death I threw myself into 'Women for Change' with renewed vigour. Like all the things in life that are of any value, it is taking a lot of hard work and determination. The beauty of this project is that it will turn around the evil forces that impacted my childhood, into a force for good.

There remained one last issue that I had not dealt with, or maybe two. But they seemed to roll into one as I searched for the last piece to make my puzzle complete. How did I feel about my mother? Could I forgive her for not protecting me? My younger brother had tried over the years to restore the broken relationships that existed within our family. He told me how tearful my mother was; how even after all this time she missed me. And in the same way that it had been pricked by her friends from work, when I had left home that first time to live with my grandparents, my guilt unsettled me.

Through my brother, I arranged to meet her, in a neutral place, a hotel, late one afternoon; time for a chat and maybe dinner. The first words she said to me were

"Oh look at you, you're beautiful."

I was fifty-six and that was the first time she had ever spoken those words to me.

We chatted, covering all the easy topics, brothers, nephew, nieces, holidays and grandchildren. I think we were both chasing that elusive relationship that we had never really found as mother and daughter. I became excited at the thought that I could have a mother in my life. My sense of the word 'mother', interpreted by the way in which I loved my children, loved in the fullest, active sense of the word. It excited me, tantalised me, the thought that something could be retrieved from the devastation that was our relationship, something that I had missed all my life. Strange that even as an older woman I still wanted a mother so very much. Deliberately keeping the conversation light we were able to steer clear of anything that might spoil this new beginning.

We arranged for her to come and stay with me for a few days, and I looked forward to her visit with great excitement, planning each day to the last minute. My daughter Kate had her reservations. She candidly told me that she was angry with my parents, and would find it difficult, if not impossible to relate to either of them. I could see when they met that Kate was disturbed, and she told me later that it felt so strange, meeting her grandmother for the first time since she was a child; a woman whom she had almost come to hate, with whom she felt she could never have any bond, and yet she had experienced, like me, a rush of emotion; a natural granddaughter/grandmother attachment.

Sadly the visit was not a success. Whichever way I tried to steer the conversation, it seemed that she would bring it back to my father – his ill health, his drinking, and the various problems that she had with him. Each time I changed the subject, each time it came back. Round and round in a big circle, sometimes stepping tentatively towards the centre, but immediately retreating back to the safer ground around the edge. My claims of the abuse sat between us like a heap of rotting vegetation. We both knew it was there, but each for different reasons did not wish to touch it.

Once I tried, raised it briefly, carefully, needing to air it, intuitively knowing that we had to clear the debris if we were to have any chance of a new relationship. But I saw her shudder, and she muttered,

"I didn't know. If I had…"

And the sentence trailed off. I knew I could not force the awful truth upon this now frail old lady. Did she know or not? I don't think that question will ever be answered. How could she ever admit to such a dreadful knowledge? But I knew it would be impossible for me to just leave it sitting on the table between us, and have a normal relationship. To let her simply ignore it and move on would be in essence a denial that it happened, and I could never countenance that.

I saw her once more at my brother's house, and we barely spoke a word to each other. He told me that when he drove her home she said,

"There's nothing there is there, nothing between me and Jacki?"

"I'm afraid not mum," was his reply.

And so the issue of forgiveness raised its ugly head. Discussing this with two members of the pastoral team at church, I was told that I must forgive, that until I did, God would not forgive me my sins. I wasted many months struggling with this, convincing myself that God expected me to forgive my parents – not only forgive them but to pick up the pieces and form a normal relationship with them. For the first time in a long while, I became depressed. I can see the pattern now, denying my own true feelings, forcing myself into a situation that I did not want because I thought it would please another, even though 'another' in this case, was God. I was repressing my own wishes, my still very strong need to tell my parents how much they had damaged me, with the result that I became frustrated, tearful and then angry.

Once again I turned to Eileen and Barbara. I poured out my heart to them, explaining that I could not forgive, that forgiving meant saying that it was all right, that what had been done to me could be forgotten, and we could all be 'happy ever after'. I knew that this would be allowing them to abuse me over and over again, every time I saw them, every time I spoke to them. If someone strikes you, turn the other cheek and let him or her do it again. My every nerve screamed "No".

When we are hurt, we hang onto it. We display it; we believe that if we continue to feel our anger and bitterness, continue to hate the person responsible for our hurt, we are punishing them. We are not, we are punishing ourselves, carrying the burden of their crime; we are allowing them to hurt us over and over again. Each and every time we think of the issue, the episode, the crime, each and every time we re-live it, we are hurting ourselves, not them.

I spent two full days with Eileen and Barbara, and their prayers and loving understanding allowed me to let this final issue go. They explained that I could not forgive in my own strength; it was too much to ask of anyone. They explained that forgiving did not mean saying that what had happened no longer mattered. It did matter, very much. Gently, and lovingly they led me to hand my parents over to God. Visually, I placed them on a tray and handed it up to him. The forgiveness was His to give, through me if and when I was ready, but in handing them over to Him I was letting go of them, releasing the final burden of bitterness, anger and guilt, putting it back, through Him, where it belonged. And no, He did not expect me to have a normal relationship with them. Finally, I could walk away from my parents. Walk away, empty handed, taking no guilt or bitterness or anger with me.

Some months later, on a sunny day, laying on a sofa in my conservatory reading my bible, I felt my heart swell, filling with a certain understanding, and I told my God that I could forgive my parents, that they were in His hands now, and I knew that I would no more have to carry their burden. The last of the emotional baggage had been unpacked.

THE KEY

She carries her burden
Throughout her life

It weighs her down
It curves her shoulders
Downcast eyes
Demeanour dragging
Along the ground
In the dirt
A victim mentality
I'm easy to hurt

Bitterness
Anger
Hurt and betrayal
Guilt and fear
So heavy
So tiring
Draining her soul

She wears them each day
Like a badge of honour
Proud to display
She keeps the anger
Alive
Lets the bitterness
Thrive
Both feed on the hurt
To repay the sin

Holding on
She cherishes the pain
Building a prison
Where she will remain
Locked in

A sentence so harsh
Self imposed?
Their gain
Her loss

She will never be free
'Til she lets them go
'Til she hunts for the key
To the doorway through
To a new life beyond

The key has a name
Not 'Forgive'
Nor 'Forget'

But

Its name is 'Love'

"Put down your burden
Let it rest with Me"

Its name is 'Freedom'

"Open the door
To your gloomy cage
Turn away from the dark
Of your captive pain
Let Me hold their guilt
Your hurt and your rage"

Its name is 'Release'

"Feel the beat of your heart
Feel the pulse of new life
Lift your eyes to the sky
You can run
You can fly"

The key has a name

Its name is 'Forever'

"I will care for you
I will love you
My gift is peace"

CHAPTER 41

Next year I shall be sixty.

I have surmounted my childhood pain, turning it into a powerful force for good in Women for Change. I have three wonderful children, and three beautiful grandchildren. My home is a haven of peace, through whose doors many people come, people who love me very much. Yes of course, I have wobbles, and I know that there will always be little hitches, trips and falls. But that is life. Life forces circumstances onto us, and we have to make choices. The choices we make are never wrong, just decisions, made in the present moment of understanding, choices which, if made on another day, in a different light, may have taken us along another road. And these choices are our responsibility. We can choose to be strong. Or not.

The foundation that my guardians gave me was built on fault lines. Distorted relationships, belittling, degrading treatment, building within me a self-image that was inferior, negative and even containing a degree of self-loathing. An innate strength, a touch of rebellion, carried me through. Caring people; grandparents and friends supported and picked me off the floor when I needed it. Was it simply the luck of the chemical draw, or fate, or the hand of God that gave me my strengths, and steered me through this precarious route to the place I am at today? Who knows?

I do know that, even given the chance, I wouldn't change one moment, not one single thing. For I love who I am now, and the reasons I am the person I am, are held within this story of my life. I am bound and formed by all the events, good and bad, that are me.

My daughter Kate is expecting her first baby – eleven days before my 60th birthday. Some weeks ago she arrived rather late at my house after having her 20-week scan. She walked into my kitchen and looked at me, her eyes shining:

"Mum, it's a girl!"

And my heart burst. Overwhelmed with joy, tears flowing freely, I hugged her, kissed her. I felt that I had been given another chance. We looked at each other, both knowing each other's thoughts, but it was Kate who dared speak the words:

"This time, we'll get it right mum."

Life is a wonderful, exciting and exhilarating journey that we take from the moment we are born until the day we die. We are handed a one-way ticket, there are no opportunities to turn back. So at every twist and turn, expected or not, shocking or pleasurable, we must endeavour to choose to hang on and enjoy the ride.